"It is perhaps the most fraught question of our time: Whatever happened to the anti-war movement? In an era of forever wars, when the body counts of civilians mount daily in countries most Americans can't spell or pinpoint on a map; when the expenditures for war-making and weaponry devour ever-larger chucks of the federal budget, miring the country in debt and foreclosing the opportunity to invest in deepening social and environmental crises, why have the once robust and rowdy voices for peace gone silent? In this provocative and illuminating book, Joan Roelofs penetrates deep into the inner-workings of the vast political economy of war-making, revealing how the arms cartel has consolidated its power, captured our political system, infiltrated the media and stifled dissent. At a perilous moment in history, Roelofs has given us a call to action, loud and clear enough to awaken our anesthetized consciences."

JEFFREY ST. CLAIR, Editor of *CounterPunch*,
author of *Grand Theft Pentagon*

"*The Trillion Dollar Silencer* is a masterful primer on an institution—the United States military—that has literally thousands of facets and functions, and about a thousand billion dollars each year to support its role in preparing for and making war around the world. Rich in explanatory images, charts and maps, the pieces of the puzzle that Joan Roelofs identifies are so many and so complex that even the most informed readers will learn something in every chapter. The book's central question is how the military industrial complex has been able to acquire so many taxpayer dollars year after year and so much cultural assent to its overwrought, violent mission. The answers she gives will help us to reverse our otherwise continuing deadly and expensive course."

CATHARINE LUTZ, Professor Emerita
of Anthropology and International Studies,
Co-Director, Costs of War Project, Brown University

"The world's leading weapons dealer and warmaker, the United States, may also have the least popular resistance to militarism. Why the quiet acceptance? This book helps us to become aware that darn near every inch of U.S. society has been infiltrated by the normalization or celebration of war preparations, that essentially our culture, not just our elected officials, has been bought. This book also provides guidance on what we can do about it."

DAVID SWANSON, Executive Director of
World Beyond War, author of *War Is A Lie*

MORE PRAISE

"Roelofs's culling of authoritative sources advocating the actual goals and tactics of the U.S. war machine—particularly those of our "unconventional warfare" policies—make it clear that any person of good conscience must oppose virtually every aspect of our country's militarized foreign policy. This book's focus is not on military and foreign policy, but rather on a question about our domestic society: Why is there so much acceptance of, and so little protest against, our war policies and all the other tactics of subversion employed by the military-intelligence-industrial complex to sustain hegemony? While the peace movement answers this question with reference to propaganda, fear and distractions, this book focuses on the enormity of the war machine's penetration into numerous aspects of civilian life. The sections on this penetration into philanthropy, nonprofit organizations, and NGOs are probably the most eye-popping of the book. Roelofs shows that the real goal is the construction of 'the normal' in ways functional to the interests of the Pentagon, unconventional warfare institutions, and military contractors."

PAUL SHANNON, Executive Committee of
Mass[achusetts] Peace Action

THE TRILLION DOLLAR
SILENCER

Why There Is So Little Anti-War
Protest in the United States

JOAN ROELOFS

Clarity Press, Inc.

ISBN: 978-1-949762-58-7
EBOOK ISBN: 978-1-949762-62-4

In-house editor: Diana G. Collier
Book design: Becky Luening

Library of Congress Control Number: 2022941863

Clarity Press, Inc.
2625 Piedmont Rd. NE, Ste. 56
Atlanta, GA 30324, USA
https://www.claritypress.com

CONTENTS

INTRODUCTION

Why is there so much acceptance of and so little protest against our government's illegal and immoral wars and other military operations? Why is there mostly silence about the death and destruction that wars and even the preparation for war inflict on people, including the troops, and on the environment? Why is there so little concern about the potential for the extinction of human and other life posed by nuclear war, now seen as an "option" by the U.S. and other militaries? While propaganda, fear, and distractions are some of the reasons, the *interests* created by military's penetration into so many aspects of civilian life is largely ignored. This book is an attempt to make visible the enormity of this penetration and the interests concerned.[1]

THE MILITARY INDUSTRIAL COMPLEX

Eisenhower's *Farewell Address to the Nation* warned as far back as 1961 of this problematic development:

This conjunction of an immense military establishment and a large arms industry is new in the American experience. The total influence—economic, political, even spiritual—is felt in every city, every Statehouse, every office of the Federal government. We recognize the imperative need for this development. Yet we must not fail to comprehend its grave implications. Our toil, resources and livelihood are all involved; so is the very structure of our society. In the councils of government, we must guard against the acquisition of unwarranted influence, whether sought or unsought, by the military-industrial complex. The potential for the disastrous rise of misplaced power exists, and will persist.[2]

1

Today Eisenhower would be amazed at how far and deeply the military-industrial complex has penetrated.

THE USE OF FORCE: ILLEGAL AND IMMORAL

The United Nations Charter, a ratified treaty and hence for the United States the "law of the land," outlaws the use of force among nations, except as approved by UN intervention resolutions or in immediate self-defense. It also prohibits non-violent aggression in any form, such as blockades, or regime change operations. These principles of the Charter have been affirmed by the UN General Assembly, inter alia in the 1981 Declaration on the Inadmissibility of Intervention and Interference in the Internal Affairs of States. Here are some excerpts:

> No State or group of States has the right to intervene or interfere in any form or for any reason whatsoever in the internal and external affairs of other States.
>
> The duty of a State [is] to refrain from the promotion, encouragement or support, direct or indirect, of rebellious or secessionist activities within other States, under any pretext whatsoever, or any action which seeks to disrupt the unity or to undermine or subvert the political order of other States;
>
> The duty of a State [is] to refrain from the exploitation and the distortion of human rights issues as a means of interference in the internal affairs of States, of pressure on other States or creating distrust and disorder within and among States or groups of States.[3]

NATO bombing of Belgrade, 1999   Source: J. Roelofs graphic

In addition, the General Assembly Declaration on Principles of International Law, Friendly Relations and Co-operation among States in Accordance with the Charter of the United Nations of 1970 provides that:

> States shall accordingly seek early and just settlement of their international disputes by negotiation, inquiry, mediation, conciliation, arbitration, judicial settlement, resort to regional agencies or arrangements or other peaceful means of their choice. In seeking such a settlement the parties shall agree upon such peaceful means as may be appropriate to the circumstances and nature of the dispute.[4]

Nevertheless, the U.S. public, press, and politicians appear unperturbed by the U.S. military conducting wars, regime change and other aggressive interventions. The North Atlantic Treaty Organization (NATO), a strong arm of the U.S. military, began its out of area wars with the bombing of Yugoslavia. There was no audible protest from U.S. citizens, which signaled a go-ahead for future illegal wars and devastations. At election time there are barely any questions to candidates on these matters reported in the media, if indeed they were raised.

Sirte, Libya, 2012
Source: Etienne Laurent, ©ECHO/European Commission 2012[5]

Even those from whom we would expect some protest—liberals, progressives, religious communities, universities, artists, civil rights organizations, and environmental activists—are strangely silent. Protest on other issues is rampant, but the outraged and discontented rarely connect their concerns to militarism, or the perpetual "war on terror." Peace activists have made a plea to those who make art on other vital issues to pay more attention to the threat of nuclear war:

> On the darker side, we have to acknowledge that much less attention is being given to the most imminent threat of all— the development, storing, selling, and transporting of nuclear weapons. ... [W]e progressives must enhance our work by incorporating the arts in our efforts to resist calls to arms and promote not just the pursuit of peace but the elimination of nuclear weapons.[6]

WHY THE SILENCE?

While much is due to propaganda, fear, and distractions, this book will focus on the interests created by the military penetration of civilian society and the domestic economy. There are other silencers of great importance, but they have already been explored in many fine publications, such as Norman Solomon's book on the media and government, *War Made Easy*.[7]

The Propaganda Blanket

From our earliest education to the contemporary culture we experience today in adulthood, we have been told that the United States is a beacon to the world and that its foreign policy is always intended for good. Very many want to believe this and do, including those who benefit from government provision and are grateful for their relative advantages, breeding a reluctance to scrutinize too closely the full scope of our government's activities. In addition, many have been persuaded that patriotism requires acceptance of whatever foreign policies the government pursues.

Our citizens do not want to believe that the U.S. government has ever engaged in war crimes. They are reassured by *Polygraph.info*, an official website that corrects what it bills as misleading foreign accusations. In response to foreign "disinformation," as an instance, we are told that "According to the U.S. Centers for Disease Control and Prevention, the United States has never used chemical weapons in warfare."[8] This, despite the overwhelming evidence of the use of napalm in Korea, Vietnam and other wars.

We hear from the media and our government that only "sissies" pay attention to international law or the UN Charter; once the derogatory epithet was "pointy-headed intellectuals" who were the spoilsports. Children are now exposed to a culture of violence and the increasing militarization of their schools, normalizing violent policies for them, much like their ubiquitous war-related computer games that teach children that killing is fun. The government, the print and digital press, TV, movies, sports shows, parades, and computer games all relentlessly promote and glorify the military.

This indoctrination is easily swallowed, since it meshes with an educational system that glorifies the violent history of the nation. Our schools are full of in-house tutoring, STEM (science, technology, engineering and mathematics) programs, and fun robotics teams personally conducted by employees of the weapons makers. Young children may not understand all the connections, but they tend to remember the logos. The JROTC programs, imparting militaristic values, enroll far more children than those who go on to become future officers. The extremely well-funded recruitment efforts in schools include "fun" simulations of warfare.

Celebrities are deployed in the propaganda; take the "Soldier for a Day" program:

> Some special guests are getting to immerse themselves in that life this weekend at remote Fort Irwin, California. From sun-up to sun-down, actors, heads of talent agencies and leaders from business giants like Lucas Oil and the NFL Network will no longer be themselves—they'll be privates, learning all there is to know about Army life.[9]

Intellectuals may be influenced by articles in "liberal" magazines alleging that violence is genetically implanted in humans and is generally a positive force. This barrage normalizes violence and war. Wanting to be regarded as normal, and not fuzzy idealists or crackpots, they can

Rockstar Energy Drink Extreme athletes   Source: DoD

comfortably view aggression as inevitable, and perhaps a good thing. The astounding notion that it is possible to bomb people into democracy is never framed as such, and overthrowing governments is presumed to be a routine world improvement activity.

In addition to a host of Department of Defense and military contractor employees whose job is "public relations," there is a worldwide supporting cast for that function, including think tanks, NATO, and foreign defense ministries and military corporations.

Fear of Reprisal

Being an outspoken opponent of war or organizing anti-war protests can incur penalties. These may range from social ostracism to loss of employment. Professors at even supposedly liberal colleges and universities have lost their positions because of opposition to U.S. foreign policy. In academia today there are fewer with any job protection and thus have much to fear. Liberal religious groups face declining memberships, and fear discouraging prospective congregants by promoting a dissenting stance. There also lurks the threat of government reprisal to individuals and organizations.

People do not want to offend their neighbors or the community leaders of civic organizations who have military connections or work in weapons manufacturing. There is strong support from the military to persuade its retirees to engage in local politics and volunteer work. Similarly, weapons companies encourage their employees to serve in national and local charitable and progressive organizations. Democratic Party supporters may fear the further loss of funding, Congressional seats and the Presidency as the electorate veers toward the right. While advocating for more humane domestic policies, their recent Congressional candidates are notably people with backgrounds in military or intelligence. In fact, the Democrats and liberals have long been major war boosters.

Distractions

With the advent of the Covid pandemic, U.S. foreign operations were even less visible. With or without this enormous distraction, many people are preoccupied by the daily difficulties of working, keeping a job, feeding the children, preventing the house from falling down, caring for ill relatives, and all the other needs of daily existence. There is little energy left to ponder U.S. foreign activities, and if they view mainstream media reports, much of the story is omitted in any event. The mainstream media assuredly doesn't publish stories which cry out for domestic anti-war protest—at least, protest that relates to bloodshed caused by the U.S.

Then there are the more obvious distractions. Alcohol, drugs, sports, TV, celebrities, internet surfing, video games, pornography, horrible crimes, earthquakes, etc., often displace attention from foreign wars. Perhaps anti-depression drugs foster political tranquility. "Make love not war" is a fine principle, but it may also be a distraction from out-of-the-house protest activities.

Meditation and hobbies are good for clearing the mind—but do they clear too much? As Jean-Jacques Rousseau put it in his *Discourse on the Arts and Sciences:*

> Science, literature, and the arts spread flowery garlands over the iron chains of law, inducing consent without obvious coercion. Thus all memory of their natural birthright liberty is stifled; they come to love their enslavement and they are transformed into a law abiding populace. Need created the powers that be; the arts and sciences fortified them. Great nations, love talents and reward those who cultivate them![10]

Volunteer work is a humanistic response to the misery around us, yet it may crowd out action to change institutions that cause those miseries. The great wave of "service learning" requirements for high school and college students was instituted in response to the radical activism of the 1970s, following policy suggestions of the Carnegie Foundation for the Advancement of Teaching.[11] It was designed to be a diversion from movements challenging capitalism and empire. Volunteers also face the entanglement of charity and reform with the military establishment and its contractors. Sometimes these connections are barely visible, and even so it is very difficult to contest kind hearts or gift horses.

Even noble causes can distract from attention to militarism's harms. Citizens and organizations working to achieve equality and justice for all are limited in time and resources, unlike the military-industrial complex. Those trying to protect our health and environment by growing our own food, seeking out local organic food and helping farmers to grow it, keeping our communities and the planet free of harmful chemicals, and recycling waste are contributing their time and energy to important tasks for human wellbeing.

Those who are immediately threatened by deafening overflight noise or toxic military waste emissions understandably try to get the military to fulfill its mission in quieter and cleaner ways. They have hopes of gaining some peace through their protests, whereas challenging the mission itself is likely to induce public disapproval.

But inescapably, all these worthy activities leave less time and attention for protesting the ghastly environmental and human destruction resulting from wars and their preparation; development, production, testing, and transportation of weapons; war games on land, sea, and air; the militarization of space; the occupation of bases; and the threat of nuclear war.

INTERESTS, VISIBLE AND HIDDEN

Our elected representatives do not have to be bribed with campaign contributions from weapons makers to support the Department of Defense budget. They may, shockingly, be representing the actual interests of many citizens. This is possible because, as Australian political scientist David T. Smith has written: "The National Security State maintains democratic legitimacy because of the way it disperses public and private benefits while shielding ordinary Americans from the true costs of high-tech warfare."[12]

As might be expected, foremost supporters are those in the military itself: the uniformed services, active, reserve, or retired, and their families—though indeed, a portion have also been among the most prominent in antiwar activism. Although the number actually engaged in our now volunteer military is small compared to previous musters, veterans and their families, including grandchildren, are numerous, and most still venerate military service. They do not focus on the killing and destruction inevitable in wars, but on comradeship, heroism, and idealism. Studies have shown that the majority of current volunteers in our services do not apply because they want to kill and destroy, but for benefits, training, comradeship, and status.[13] These are now emphasized by recruiters, who speak low about the realities of military operations.

For veterans and all others, the military industrial complex's unbeatable weapon is jobs, and all members of Congress, and state and local officials, are aware of this. Here is where well-paying jobs are found for mechanics, scientists, and engineers; even janitorial workers do better in taxpayer-rich agencies and industries. Expanding budgets permit many new hires in all positions and the implementation of diversity goals.

The economic impact of the military-industrial complex is a highly effective silencer. While it may contribute to a vastly unjust distribution of resources domestically, it also helps to keep the sagging economy afloat. Although current government expenditure (state, local, and federal) for education, health care, highways, other infrastructure, social security, and welfare far outweighs military expenditures, there is little doubt that, for a state claiming to provide global leadership and example, these sectors are severely underfunded.

Military spending is about 10% of all government outlays, but it consumes more than half of the federal government discretionary budget.[14]

This type of spending has a great impact on the economy because:

- it is a growing sector;
- it is recession-proof;
- it does not rely on consumer whims;
- it is a boon in rusted and depressed areas of the country;
- it is ideally suited to Keynesian remedies, because of the ready destruction and obsolescence of its products—what isn't consumed in warfare, rusted out, or donated to our many allies still needs to be replaced by the slightly more lethal versions concocted in our research labs;
- the "multiplier" effect: contractors, subcontractors, corporate purchasing, and employee spending, as well as military bases and

installations, are economic hubs of their region. supplying customers for real estate agents, landscapers, restaurants, tap dancing
schools, furniture shops, museums, and yoga studios;

• local governments' enhanced tax receipts support social services,
  education, infrastructure, and culture.

The appropriators in Congress are well aware of these benefits to
their districts, along with their other incentives for generous funding
such as campaign contributions and lobbying. Congresspeople also
hold weapons industry stocks; some are gifts from lobbyists. When
legal limits of campaign donations are reached, or for laundering their
provenance, military corporations' "foundations" donate to charities in
Congresspeople's districts.

Weaponry is also an important share of U.S. manufactured goods
exports; our allies are required to have equipment that meets U.S. spec-
ifications. In addition to economic benefits, foreign purchases enable
weapon testing in diverse terrains. In any case, other governments, reb-
els, terrorists, pirates, and gangsters all fancy our high tech and low-tech
devices.

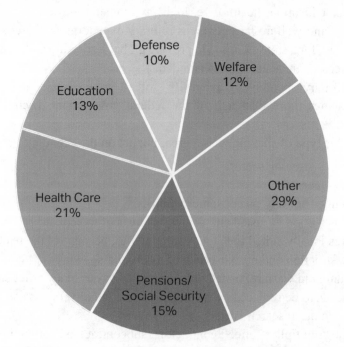

All Government Spending (2020)   Source: Wikipedia Commons

Estimate of U.S. Post-9/11 War Spending, in $ Billions FY2001-FY2022

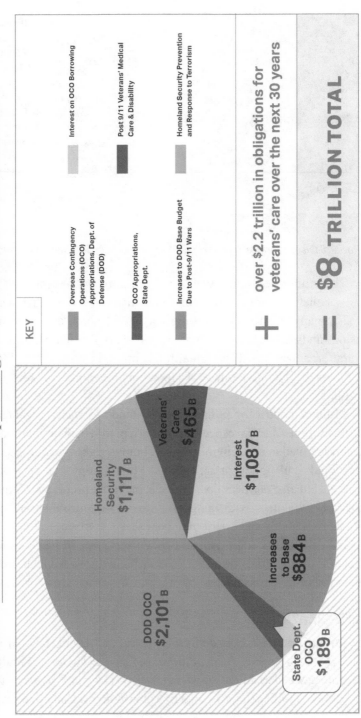

Budgetary Costs of War

Source: Costs of War Project[15]

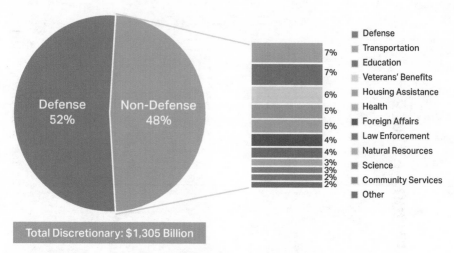

	■ Defense
7%	■ Transportation
7%	■ Education
	■ Veterans' Benefits
6%	■ Housing Assistance
5%	■ Health
5%	■ Foreign Affairs
4%	■ Law Enforcement
4%	■ Natural Resources
3%	■ Science
3%	
2%	■ Community Services
2%	■ Other

Total Discretionary: $1,305 Billion

Federal Discretionary Spending (2019)   Source: Wikipedia Commons

The military economy yields a high return on investments. These returns benefit not only corporate executives and the other wealthy, but also many middle and working class folk; union and civil service pension funds; churches; universities; and charitable, human rights, and cultural organizations. The mutual funds offered by Vanguard, Fidelity, and others are lucrative due to weapons manufacturers' stocks in their portfolios.

Military contractor philanthropy extends to many organizations and institutions and is especially attentive to youth and minorities. Support is given to arts, environmental, human rights, health, disability, educational, and policy organizations. Philanthropy confers not only donations but also partnerships, projects, and joint programs. Contractor employees volunteer with nongovernmental organizations and public schools; executives and board members serve as trustees of nonprofits. Thus, our defunded and privatized social services, arts, and education systems are benefitting from the federal budget in a backhanded way, with strings and logos attached.

MILITARIZATION

Militarization has been defined by historian Richard H. Kohn as "the degree to which a society's institutions, policies, behaviors, thought, and values are devoted to military power and shaped by war."[16] It also signifies an ideology of militarism, as stated by anthropologist Catherine Lutz:

[That] entails seeing the world as a series of threats to be dealt with, sorting people into enemies and allies, and focusing on the use or threat of force—physical (missile and machine gun fire), mental (psychological operations, public relations campaigns) and financial (enforcement of sanctions, bribery of local actors, arms deals).[17]

Militarization is also reflected in the blurring of the boundaries between military and civilian institutions, projects, and culture. This is not new in United States history, as from the outset of our nation, the Army Corps of Engineers built forts and ports. After the Civil War the assembly line processes of the weapons manufacturers became the model for civilian industries.

The federal land-grant program (Morrill Act) funding colleges and universities specified military technology as part of the curricula. The National Guard has long been involved in civilian administration, most obviously in disaster relief, which brings many civilian humanitarians into its orbit. More recently, the Guard has served in vaccination programs and as essential workers, for example, public school teachers, to replace those too ill to work.

Our society has not approached the extreme militarization of ancient Sparta; nevertheless, there is serious concern:

[M]ilitaristic societies generally do not require boys to be physically separated from their families to be transformed into soldiers. Instead, it is more common for the contemporary national security state to reach into all aspects of life. In the contemporary United States, spending on war and defense is generally unquestioned; economic life is tightly tied to the imperatives of war-making, war preparedness, and national "security"; and popular culture is saturated with entertainment—video games, tv programs, films—that glorify and normalize militarism.[18]

Militarization was always part of United States (and Colonial) culture, yet the Enlightenment and religious enthusiasm created a respectable pacifist counterculture in the 19th Century. There was a sharp turn in the atmosphere with World War I, when soldiering was glorified and pacifism was no longer a respectable orientation—indeed, many pacifists were jailed or suffered other serious consequences. The subsequent Depression and preparation for another war began large-scale blurring of the boundaries between the military and civil society. The massive electrification project of the Tennessee Valley Authority brought genuine benefits to many, especially women whose lives were transformed by electrified laundry machines. However, hydroelectricity was also intended to provide more efficient weapons production, particularly at the munitions plant at Muscle Shoals, Alabama. Eventually, the TVA and similar projects damming the Columbia River in the Northwest became instrumental for nuclear weapon production.

The mobilization for World War II and the subsequent Cold War brought universities, industries, and many civilian institutions into partnerships with the warfare state. Nevertheless, in 1941 it was still possible for Congress (the Truman Committee) to investigate corruption in war contracting and thereby shed some light on the military-industrial complex.

The Vietnam War and the revelations of CIA covert actions produced a loud counterculture of protest. The collaboration of universities, civic and professional organizations, and unions was decried, but these voices were soon diminished. Seymour Melman's *The Permanent War Economy* (1976) was a revelation and a warning. However, despite the past protests related to particular wars, a strong demilitarization movement has not yet evolved. "Even though American society is increasingly shaped by the economic, media, and political effects of war, there has been a scarcity of comprehensive plans to escape from a permanent war society."[19]

Militarization can proceed without much public notice as its outlines are blurred. This applies as well to the low visibility of unconventional warfare, particularly Special Forces operations. Regrettably, the attack on U.S. soil on September 11, 2001, and the subsequent "war on terror" gave ammunition to the advocates of a permanent war economy.

Increasing militarization is a worldwide phenomenon, somewhat surprisingly so in the social democracies of Western Europe. Antiwar activists are louder there than in the United States, but they haven't had much influence on political parties or parliaments. Weapons industries and foreign sales are economically important in many European countries, where, like the United States, civilian manufacturing has been mostly outsourced. Institutions created or aided by the U.S., especially NATO, have led to a network able to overpower the peace advocates. This is reinforced by military sales and aid, military training, joint operation forces, and bases. Even countries reputedly neutral, such as Sweden, are partners of NATO, and the alliance has affiliates on all continents.

As the imitation of American ways gradually pervades the world, it creates a more congenial setting for the exercise of the indirect and seemingly consensual American hegemony. And as in the case of the domestic American system, that hegemony involves a complex structure of interlocking institutions and procedures, designed to generate consensus and obscure asymmetries in power and influence.[20]

ABOUT THIS BOOK

This book describes a labyrinthine array of organizations, departments, agencies, boards, and partnerships involving government, industry, universities, and nonprofits. It may seem complicated with the information overlapping, but these collaborations are of great significance. For all its low visibility—even because of it—this is how our governance system has evolved. While the phenomenon is not new, patronage relationships and networks have increasingly overpowered the potentially democratic system of political parties and elections. Elected representatives are either persons of great wealth, or primarily agents of their financial sponsors.[21] There are a few who are advocates for the people, in some special areas of the country, but they must compromise a lot to get a little, and even fewer find it politic to confront the military. Nongovernmental organizations are among the lobbyists, and they can get a piece of the pie if they don't rock the boat.

A report, *Recent Social Trends in the United States*, financed by the Rockefeller Foundation, was presented to President Hoover in 1933.[22] It was a response to the Great Depression and to long-standing dysfunctions in United States society and economy. Among the new governance structures it advocated were quasi-governmental entities and public-private corporations; the Tennessee Valley Authority is a prime example. The current economic development corporations—there is a federal one as well as a multitude of state and local ones—are excellent examples of the sinews between the military budget and our economy. These relationships are quite visible to politicians, public administrators, and civic leaders. Making them visible to a wider audience may not disrupt the growing militarization of the United States, but surely recognition and explanation are required before an effective way to confront it can be found.

NOTES

The appearance of U.S. Department of Defense (DoD) visual information does not imply or constitute DoD endorsement.

1 A book that covers some of the same ground, but from an insider perspective, is Rosa Brooks, *How Everything Became War and the Military Became Everything: Tales from the Pentagon* (New York: Simon & Schuster, 2016).
2 "President Dwight D. Eisenhower's Farewell Address (1961)," National Archives, https://www.archives.gov/milestone-documents/president-dwight-d-eisenhowers-farewell-address.
3 *Declaration on the Inadmissibility of Intervention and Interference in the Internal Affairs of States* (1982), United Nations Digital Library, https://digitallibrary.un.org/record/27066?ln=en.
4 *Declaration on Principles of International Law concerning Friendly Relations and Cooperation among States in accordance with the Charter of the United Nations* (New York, October 24, 1970), Audiovisual Library of International Law, https://legal.un.org/avl/ha/dpilfrscun/dpilfrscun.html.
5 Etienne Laurent [copyright 2012 ECHO/European Commission], January 23, 2012, EU Civil Protection and Humanitarian Aid photostream, *Flickr,* https://www.flickr.com/photos/eu_echo/6879903205/. Original caption: "ECHO/DDG - Mine clearance Sirte: After two months of heavy fighting between revolutionaries and the pro regime army, the city of Sirte is in ruin. With an unknown number of ammunition used during the conflict, the number of unexploded ordnances scattered all over the city is enormous and represent a threat for people. The Danish Demining Group, financed by ECHO, is disarming these UXOs."
6 André de Quadros and Kathie Malley-Morrison, "Artists Unite Against Nuclear Annihilation," *Peace Advocate* (Massachusetts Peace Action, February 2022), https://masspeaceaction.org/artists-unite-against-nuclear-annihilation/
7 Norman Solomon, *War Made Easy* (New York: Wiley, 2006).
8 Fatima Tlis, "Olympic Obfuscation: At Games: China-Russia Jab U.S. on Chemical Weapons," *Polygraph.info* (Feb. 9, 2022), https://www.polygraph.info/a/fact-check-xi-putin/31693558.html.
9 Katie Lange, "Ever Want to Be a Soldier? Some VIPs Get the Chance for a Day," *MilSpouseFest* (November 16, 2017), https://stg.milspousefest.com/ever-want-to-be-a-soldier-some-vips-get-the-chance-for-a-day/.
10 Jean-Jacques Rousseau, *The First and Second Discourses* (New York: St. Martin's Press, 1964), 36.

11 *Carnegie Review: A New Civic Mission of Schools* (Carnegie Corporation of New York, Spring 2011), https://media.carnegie.org/filer_public/85/8b/858b7e5d-c538-42e2-ae78-24471dce73d7/ccny_creview_2011_civic.pdf.

12 David T. Smith, "From the Military-industrial Complex to the National Security State," *Australian Journal of Political Science*, Vol. 50, No. 3 (September 2015): 576–590.

13 Jared Keller, "The Top 5 Reasons Soldiers Really Join The Army, According To Junior Enlisted," *Task and Purpose*, May 14, 2018. https://taskandpurpose.com/joining-the-military/5-reasons-soldiers-join-army/

14 *usgovernmentspending.com*, https://www.usgovernmentspending.com/year_spending_2020USbt_21bs2n#usgs302; *National Priorities Project*, https://www.nationalpriorities.org/

15 Neta C. Crawford, "The U.S. Budgetary Costs of the Post-9/11 Wars." Costs of War Project, Watson Institute for International and Public Affairs, Brown University, September 1, 2021. Graphic designed by Maria Ji. https://watson.brown.edu/costsofwar/figures/2021/BudgetaryCosts,

16 Roberto J. González, Hugh Gusterson, and Gustaaf Houtman (eds.), *Militarization: A Reader* (Durham: Duke University Press, 2019), 6.

17 Catherine Lutz, "Selling ourselves? The Perils of Pentagon Funding for Anthropology," *Anthropology Today*, Vol. 24, No. 5 (October 2008): 2.

18 González et al., *Militarization*, 12.

19 Jonathan Feldman, "From Warfare State to 'Shadow State': Militarism, Economic Depletion, and Reconstruction," *Social Text*, Vol. 25, No. 2 (Summer 2007): 155.

20 Zbigniew Brzezinski, *The Grand Chessboard* (New York: Basic Books, 1997), 27.

21 Martin Gilens & Benjamin I. Page, "Testing Theories of American Politics: Elites, Interest Groups, and Average Citizens," *Perspectives on Politics*, Vol. 12, No. 3, (Sept. 2014): 564–81.

22 President's Research Committee on Social Trends, *Recent Social Trends in the United States* [1933], 2 vols. (Greenwood: Westport, 1970).

CHAPTER ONE

THE MILITARY ESTABLISHMENT

THE MALIGNANCY OF WAR

Of all the enemies of true liberty, war is, perhaps, the most to be dreaded, because it comprises and develops the germ of every other. War is the parent of armies; from these proceed debts and taxes; and armies and debts and taxes are the known instruments for bringing the many under the domination of the few. In war, too, the discretionary power of the Executive is extended; its influence in dealing out offices, honors and emoluments is multiplied; and all the means of seducing the minds, are added to those of subduing the force of the people.

The same malignant aspect in republicanism may be traced in the inequality of fortunes, and the opportunities of fraud, growing out of a state of war, and in the degeneracy of manner and of morals, engendered in both. No nation can preserve its freedom in the midst of continual warfare.

—James Madison, "Political Observations," 1795[1]

Nevertheless, as President, Madison requested that Congress declare war against Britain, initiating the War of 1812,[2] and during his administration the American Indian Wars continued: Tecumseh's War, the Creek War, and the First Seminole War.[3]

WORLD EFFORTS PROMOTING PEACE

The horrific death, disease, and destruction of the U.S. Civil War and the 19th century European wars inspired the Geneva Convention of 1864. It provided for the treatment of the wounded, and prohibited the use of poisons, the killing of enemy combatants who have surrendered, looting of a town or place, and the attack or bombardment of undefended towns or habitations. It stated that inhabitants of occupied territories could not be forced into military service against their own country and forbade collective punishment. The International Committee of the Red Cross was to monitor and assist in its enforcement. Major European powers signed this Convention and the United States joined in 1882.

The Hague Peace Conference of 1899 was convened at the initiative of the Czar of Russia, Nicholas II, "with the object of seeking the most effective means of ensuring to all peoples the benefits of a real and lasting peace, and, above all, of limiting the progressive development of existing armaments." Many hoped it would abolish war forever, by providing for peaceful means of resolving international disputes. It did succeed in establishing a Permanent Court of Arbitration, which still exists. It also resulted in conventions and declarations that reiterated the earlier Geneva Convention and provided more rules for the conduct of war and the prohibition of particularly gruesome armaments. The Second Hague Conference, in 1907, created additional treaties.

Hague Conference 1907   Source: Creative Commons

The Geneva Conventions of 1949 enlarged upon the rules, and came to be known as international humanitarian law. Several treaties now prohibit the most obnoxious armaments. The U.S. has ratified some of these treaties, often with stated exceptions or failure to implement.[4]

World War I dashed the hopes for peace and most rules of war, yet in 1928 the Kellogg-Briand Pact was signed. This treaty between the

United States and most nations of the world called for the renunciation of war as an instrument of national policy. It is still part of our law but has not generally been enforced. In 1945 the United States ratified another important treaty, the Charter of the United Nations. Article 2 states:

> All Members shall settle their international disputes by peaceful means. . . . All Members shall refrain in their international relations from the threat or use of force against the territorial integrity or political independence of any state, or in any other manner inconsistent with the Purposes of the United Nations.[5]

The Nuremberg Principles of 1947 were guidelines for future treaties; some nations accept them as customary international law. They include crimes against peace; planning, preparation, initiation or waging of a war of aggression or a war in violation of international treaties, agreements or assurances; and participation in a common plan or conspiracy for the accomplishment of any of these acts. The International Criminal Court (ICC), which began its work in 2002, "investigates and, where warranted, tries individuals charged with the gravest crimes of concern to the international community: genocide, war crimes, crimes against humanity and the crime of aggression."[6] The U.S. has not signed or ratified the ICC treaty.

UNITED STATES POLICY

The U.S. Constitution, Article VI, states in part: "This Constitution, and the laws of the United States which shall be made in pursuance thereof; and all treaties made, or which shall be made, under the authority of the United States, shall be the supreme law of the land; . ." The Constitution also provides for Congress "To declare War, and To raise and support Armies, but no Appropriation of Money to that Use shall be for a longer Term than two Years." The War Powers Act of 1973 was enacted to limit the President's power to make war without a declaration or approval of Congress, but it has not proven very effective in restraining U.S. aggression. In practice, Congress has not been inclined to use any of its powers to prevent U.S. violations of international law.

Although the United States played a major role in creating the United Nations, and ratified the UN Charter, it immediately countered its intent with the Truman Doctrine of 1947, which proclaimed that the U.S. will intervene in any way, including militarily, in any place where communism threatens, either by outside pressures or domestic insurgents.[7] The context was the civil war in Greece; Truman requested and received the go-ahead for economic and military intervention. Napalm was used against the Greek Communists, along with covert operations to create a compliant regime. The Truman doctrine was even extended to situations where elections might result in communist governments.

In 1950 the National Security Council issued a policy document, known as NSC-68, which was a blueprint for the Cold War, proposing a massive military buildup to "rollback" communism where it existed and to prevent any additional nations from adopting communist governments. All means were implied, including covert action, military intervention, and pre-emptive nuclear war. This remains our operative policy: the U.S. president may order a pre-emptive nuclear strike, not necessarily in retaliation, including against a non-nuclear state. The president's power as "commander in chief" survives from our 18th century Constitution, a time when monarchs led troops into battle.

Eisenhower's "Farewell Address to the Nation" in 1961, warning of the influence of the military-industrial complex, did not slow down the militarization of U.S. policies and public and private institutions.[8] The Global War on Terror, announced by President George Bush in 2001, assumed no limits on U.S. intervention anywhere and in any form.

The current strategy, announced by the Department of Defense in 2018, states:

> Long-term strategic competitions with China and Russia are the principal priorities for the [Defense] Department, and require both increased and sustained investment, because of the magnitude of the threats they pose to U.S. security and prosperity today, and the potential for those threats to increase in the future. Concurrently, the Department will sustain its efforts to deter and counter rogue regimes such as North Korea and Iran, defeat terrorist threats to the United States, and consolidate our gains in Iraq and Afghanistan while moving to a more resource-sustainable approach.
>
> A more lethal, resilient, and rapidly innovating Joint Force, combined with a robust constellation of allies and

partners, will sustain American influence and ensure favorable balances of power that safeguard the free and open
international order.[9]

UNCONVENTIONAL WARFARE

Cold War covert actions, carried out by the Central Intelligence
Agency (CIA) and supported by the military, have increasingly been
adopted as the dominant strategy of the Department of Defense (DoD).
These operations have been declared successful by our leaders, and to
boot, less costly and threatening to planetary life than invasions and
nuclear warfare. They are also barely visible to U.S. citizens, and consequently less likely to be protested. Although such interventions violate
international law and our treaties, this is sidestepped by the effort to ensure that covert operations are carried out within the framework of "de-
niability," i.e. are sufficiently ambiguous or disguised so that denial can
claim credibility. In any case, the U.S. government does not recognize
international law in these gravest matters, only in innocuous provisions,
to further economic interests, or to enhance national reputation.

As Nick Turse puts it, "Today, American warfare is increasingly
typified by a reliance on Special Operations Forces (SOF), private contractors, local proxies working with and for the military and CIA, and
air power. These low-visibility forces make for greater secrecy and less
accountability."[10] The leaders of the DoD Special Operations Command
see unconventional warfare (UW), which they call "The Gray Zone," as
the wave of the present and future warfare. It is addressed in *Joint Force
Quarterly* as follows:

> The Gray Zone is characterized by intense political, economic,
> informational, and military competition more fervent in nature
> than normal steady-state diplomacy, yet short of conventional
> war. . . . small-footprint, low-visibility operations often of a
> covert or clandestine nature. . .
>
> [It is typified by] Political warfare. . . a population-cen-
> tric engagement that seeks to influence, to persuade, even to
> co-opt. One of its staunchest proponents, George Kennan,
> described it as "the employment of all the means at a nation's
> command, short of war, to achieve its national objectives,"
> including overt measures such as white propaganda, political

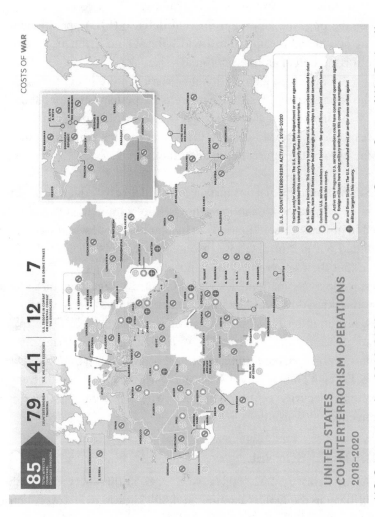

COSTS OF **WAR**

U.S. Counterterrorism 2018–2020

Source: Costs of War Project[11]

alliances, and economic programs, to "such covert operations as clandestine support of 'friendly' foreign elements, 'black' psychological warfare, and even encouragement of underground resistance in hostile states." UW can be used as a regime change mechanism, enabling an indigenous resistance or insurgent group to overthrow the existing government. . . [or the opposite:] Foreign internal defense (FID) operations are conducted to support a friendly foreign government in its efforts to defeat an internal threat.

In our era, unconventional warfare is more likely to take the form of a civil resistance movement, perhaps manipulated by foreign powers, that seeks to provoke a violent government response in order to destroy that government's legitimacy in the eyes of the international community.[12]

So, while the special ops instances are allegedly "covert," the actual U.S. policy framework enabling same is fully admitted and can be discussed in military-related journals in blatant black and white—this must be pointed out just in case any insouciant members of the public still believe that their government does not do such things. SOF engage in "high-profile assassinations, low-level targeted killings, capture/kidnap operations, kick-down-the-door night raids, joint operations with foreign forces, and training missions with indigenous partners."[13] The Special Operations Command describes its operations as "Counterinsurgency, Counterterrorism, Countering Weapons of Mass Destruction, Direct Action, Foreign Humanitarian Assistance, Military Information Support Operations, Security Force Assistance, Special Reconnaissance, and Unconventional Warfare."[14]

MILITARY PERSONNEL

As of February 2022, there were 2.91 million service members and civilians in the DoD, operating at 4,800 sites in over 160 countries around the world.[15] The services include the Army, Navy, Marine Corps, Air Force, and Space Force. The world is divided into "commands" for the U.S. military.

The Special Operations Forces (Rangers, Seals, Snipers, Green Berets, Delta Force et al) are of increasing importance. The U.S. Special

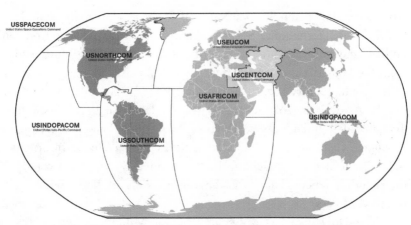

U.S. Military Commands   Source: Wikimedia

Operations Command (USSOCOM) includes about 70,000 members from active duty (from all the services), National Guard, and reserve personnel, and Department of Defense civilians.[16] The National Guard serves in state, national, and overseas missions with the SOF and other units. The Guard is frequently deployed in climate and other disasters, health emergencies, vaccination programs, and sometimes even for relief of public school teacher shortages related to COVID. "Due to the teacher shortage in New Mexico, many members of the National Guard are now working in schools. In 36 of the state's 89 school zones, or districts, Guard members are working."[17]

The DoD has about 950,000 civilian employees, engaged in 675 different occupations, and serving worldwide.[18] In addition to the services and commands, the DoD has many specialized agencies, some serving all the branches, such as the Defense Logistics Agency. The CIA cooperates with the DoD, and itself includes 18 intelligence agencies, the best-known of which is the National Security Agency. Many federal government entities work cooperatively with the DoD, from the State Department to the Fish and Wildlife Service. The Pentagon is truly labyrinthine.

MILITARY INSTITUTES

The traditional military academies, West Point, Naval Academy, and Air Force Academy and additional specialized universities and institutes are managed by the DoD. They provide degrees, courses, or training for civilians and military personnel from the U.S. and worldwide. For example, the National Defense University includes a "College of International Security Affairs . . . to educate and prepare civilian and military national security professionals and future leaders from the United States and partner nations for the strategic challenges of the contemporary security environment."[19] Among other institutions are the Army War College, Naval War College, Air Force Institute of Technology, Air University, Defense Acquisition University, Defense Language Institute, Naval Postgraduate School, Defense Information School, and a medical school, the Uniformed Services University of the Health Sciences. Faculty at these institutions are both civilians and military officers.

The DoD also has designated Senior Military Colleges, which offer a combination of higher education with military instruction. These are Texas A&M University, Norwich University, the Virginia Military Institute, The Citadel, Virginia Polytechnic Institute and State University (Virginia Tech), University of North Georgia, and the Mary Baldwin Women's Institute for Leadership. These differ from the military academies insofar as the cadets share the universities with civilian students and enroll in non-military courses offered by the regular faculty. "Every cadet must participate in the ROTC (Reserve Officers' Training Corps) program, but only those cadets who receive an ROTC scholarship are required to enter military service following graduation."[20]

Some other training sites are the Africa Center for Strategic Studies (In D.C., Senegal, and Ethiopia), U.S. Army JFK Special Warfare Center and School, Ft. Bragg, NC for Special Forces training (Green Berets), and the Western Hemisphere Institute for Security Cooperation, formerly named the U.S. Army School of the Americas, Ft. Benning, Georgia, but renamed due to its notoriety.

A large network of universities and institutes are affiliated with the North Atlantic Treaty Organization, which itself is effectively an adjunct of the U.S. military. These train U.S. and foreign troops as well as civilians who are in national defense establishments or those planning political careers in international relations or military policy. The institutions include NATO Defense College Rome, NATO School Oberammergau, NATO Communications & Information Systems School, NATO Maritime Interdiction Operational Training Center, Joint Warfare Center, Joint Force Training Center and others. Some are in countries that are "partners" but not full NATO members.[21]

RESEARCH DIVISIONS

Research agencies include the Defense Advanced Research Projects Agency (DARPA), the Defense Medical Research and Development Program, Defense Threat Reduction Agency (DTRA), the Office of Naval Research, Air Force Office of Scientific Research, U.S. Army Research Institute of Environmental Medicine (USARIEM), Readiness and Environmental Protection Integration Program, and Strategic Environmental Research and Development Program. (The latter two are discussed in Chapter 2, Bases).

The Natick Soldier Systems Center

One installation with likely repercussions on civilian life is the Natick Soldier Systems Center, a division of the Army Research Institute of Environmental Medicine. It is not far from Walden Pond, made famous by 19th Century antiwar author, Henry David Thoreau. The Natick Center "is responsible for the technology, research, development, engineering, fielding, and sustainment of our military's food, clothing, shelters, airdrop systems, and Soldier support items."[22] It also researches space rations. Here is one of its breakthroughs in 2018:

> Scientists in the Combat Feeding Directorate at the Natick Soldier Research, Development and Engineering Center have overcome the obstacles inherent in creating and producing a shelf-stable pizza to be included in the MRE [Meals, Ready-to-Eat]. . . . Most people are used to eating pizza that's fresh or frozen, but creating a pizza for the warfighter in the field, in remote areas, or in combat presents a series of unique scientific challenges. MREs must stay shelf-stable for three years in temperatures up to 80 degrees Fahrenheit. Moreover, achieving this extended shelf life with the combination of traditional pizza ingredients is particularly difficult.[23]

The Natick extensive nutritional research, such as the Military Eating Behavior Survey, interests civilian health educators. Some studies use civilian volunteers, as reflected in the following announcement:

USARIEM's nutrition researchers are seeking participants who live around the Natick, Massachusetts area and are willing to come to USARIEM's laboratory located in Natick Soldier Systems Center. Some of these studies will involve eating a military ration-based diet, which includes Meals, Ready-to-Eat, or MREs, for certain periods of time.[24]

Pizza MRE   Source: DoD U.S. Army

Food preservation and delivery processes, such as canned and pouched food, have long been pioneered by the military. However, contemporary MREs' spread into the general civilian cuisine may be a horse of a different color.

Defense Advanced Research Projects Agency

The Defense Advanced Research Projects Agency (DARPA), although mainly involved with hi-tech futuristic weapons development, also aspires to civilian applications. As an instance, it states that human populations are put at risk when food security is challenged, and therefore is undertaking a project to "Enlist Insects to Protect Agricultural Food Supply:"

A new DARPA program is poised to provide an alternative to traditional agricultural threat response, using targeted gene therapy to protect mature plants within a single growing season. DARPA proposes to leverage a natural and very efficient two-step delivery system to transfer modified genes to plants:

insect vectors and the plant viruses they transmit. In the process, DARPA aims to transform certain insect pests into "Insect Allies," the name of the new effort.

"Insects eat plants and insects transmit the majority of plant viruses," said Blake Bextine, the DARPA program manager for Insect Allies. "DARPA plans to harness the power of this natural system by engineering genes inside plant viruses that can be transmitted by insects to confer protective traits to the target plants they feed upon."[25]

Bearing in mind that DARPA is a military research agency, this seemingly benign and civilian-related project seems likely to be evolving its Insect Allies' capacities for deployment in other fields.

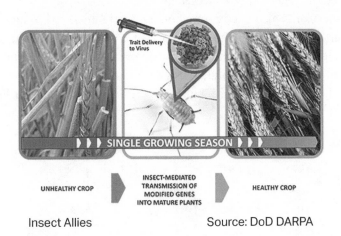

Insect Allies   Source: DoD DARPA

ARMY CORPS OF ENGINEERS

From its origin at the beginning of our nation, the Army Corps of Engineers has constructed both military and civilian works. These included coastal fortifications, mapping the American West, lighthouses, post offices, jetties and piers, and mapping navigation channels. It later engaged in flood control and the creation of hydroelectric energy. Now it is very visible as it constructs and maintains state and national parks and recreation areas.

In parks throughout the nation, the Corps sponsors a Junior Ranger program "to develop in the young people who visit Corps of Engineers lakes an awareness of the environment and the role the Corps plays in managing this environment at the lakes, and to solicit their assistance in helping Corps rangers in serving the public and protecting our lands and natural resources."[26]

The Corps continues to build military facilities both in the U.S. and abroad. "During the Cold War, Army engineers managed construction programs for America's allies, including a massive effort in Saudi Arabia."[27] Most in the Corps are civilian employees, but the military recruiters emphasize that they will be "making a direct contribution to war fighters and their families, and supporting overseas contingency operations, . . ."[28] Careers in the Corps include Ecology, Fish Biology, Wildlife Biology, Park Ranger, Biologists, Natural Resources Specialists, Engineering Technician, Architects, Environmental Engineers, and Information Technology Management.

The Corps also uses contractors and volunteers, who may "serve as a park or campground host, staff a visitor center, maintain park trails and facilities, lead tours of the lock, dam or power plant, present educational programs, clean shorelines, or restore fish and wildlife habitat."[29] The volunteers are not paid, but receive tools, training, and a free RV campsite with hookups.

Junior Rangers   Source: DoD U.S. Army

DEFENSE DEPARTMENT CIVILIAN EMPLOYEES

The civilian employees of the DoD run the gamut. The largest groups are in acquisitions, intelligence, and cyberspace operations. That said, surprisingly there are 675 different occupations. One option is the Expeditionary Civilian mission. In a program started in 2009, DOD civilian workers can deploy to war zones as "joint individual augmentees, and are placed where they're most needed in a joint-service contingency environment, including in Iraq, Afghanistan and elsewhere, to meet future global challenges."[30]

More mundane job openings listed recently include child and youth program assistant, bartender, automotive worker, attorney, forklift operator, environmental protection specialist, program analyst, equal employment specialist, wood worker, and cook.[31] There are opportunities for writers, artists, editors, archaeologists, ecologists, professors, and specialists in all fields.

DoD Public Affairs specialists can work in the U.S. and worldwide, providing print or video information, social media postings, or live demonstrations. Each branch of the military has Outreach and Community Relations agencies. The Army's office reaches out to engage the civilian population, offering its participation and services in local events in the manner below:

> Thank you for your interest in an Army aviation asset at your event. We can provide aerial tactical demonstrations and fly-overs, to include helicopter static displays at civilian air shows and local patriotic events. The Army Parachute Demonstration Teams, such as the Silver Wings (Ft. Benning), Black Daggers, (Ft. Bragg) and Screaming Eagles (Ft. Campbell) are also available on a limited local basis. The Army Golden Knights are our premier parachute demonstration team and one of our best recruiting assets. . . .
>
> Your event must meet the following criteria [among others] in order to be considered:
>
> The event or observance must be of sufficient size and significance to justify the use of Army aircraft. The event should benefit the Army, have significant community interest, and be patriotic in tone.[32]

Show business enthusiasts can serve in the Department of Defense Entertainment Media Office that "supports studios, production companies, producers, directors, screenwriters, location managers, actors, and filmmakers in the production of both scripted and unscripted films."[33]

It is estimated that the Pentagon has assisted in producing over five hundred Hollywood films since the creation of the Department of Defense in 1947. What is more surprising than the breadth of its influence, however, is the depth of its influence. The Department of Defense monitors the production of each film it supports, from start to finish. And if production departs from its vision, the Department of Defense reserves the right to withdraw at any time.[34]

Civilian workers are recruited with many internship opportunities, including the Student Temporary Education Program, the Student Career Experience Program, the Department of Defense Centralized Intern Program, the National Security Agency Graduate Training Program, and the Workforce Recruitment Program for College Students with Disabilities.

The Washington Headquarters Services offers internships in the following areas:

- IT and Network Security
- Intelligence, Acquisitions & Procurement
- Graphic Design
- Public Affairs & Communications
- Test & Evaluation, International Affairs
- Congressional Liaisons, Human Resources
- Legal (General Counsel), Defense Policy
- Administration & Management, Logistics
- Facilities Management
- Finance (Accounting, Comptroller)
- Engineering
- Economics
- Over 750 Career Areas...[35]

There are also scholarships for students at all levels, from high school to graduate fellowships, in all these fields and more, including social work, health care administration, and languages.

MILITARY PROPERTY

The most recent Base Structure Report of the DoD indicates 4,775 properties owned or leased, in the U.S., territories, and overseas.[36] Independent investigative reporters estimate that there are about 750 to 800 overseas bases, with Camp Bondsteel in Kosovo being the largest. These foreign installations, and the continuing protests against them at the Okinawa, Diego Garcia, Vicenza, and Ramstein bases, among others, have been well described in books by Joseph Gerson and Bruce Birchard, Catherine Lutz, Nick Turse, and David Vine, and in an excellent video, *Standing Army*.[37] They will not be addressed in this book, although interests benefitting from them breed silence (or support) by both U.S. and foreign citizens.

Chapter Two will consider the impacts of domestic bases. The following indicates the scope of the military occupation of our landscape:

The DoD historic property portfolio includes 49 individual National Historic Landmarks, 3,171 National Historic Landmark contributing properties, 2,396 individual and contributing historic assets listed in the National Register of Historic Places, over 15,000 historic assets determined eligible for inclusion in the National Register of Historic Places, and over 132,000 recorded archaeological sites.[38]

COOPERATING FEDERAL DEPARTMENTS

The DoD mission is furthered by collaboration with other federal departments and agencies, including the Department of Agriculture, which participated in creating a dairy cattle industry in Afghanistan. No matter that the cattle and their feed must be imported, that cattle cannot graze in the terrain as the native sheep and goats can, that there is no adequate transportation or refrigeration, and that the Afghans don't normally drink milk. The native animals provide yogurt, butter, and wool, and graze on the rugged slopes, but that is all so un-American – and independent of American products.

The Central Intelligence Agency provides a model and partner in unconventional warfare; the U.S. Agency for International Development also contributes to overseas operations. The Department of Energy is primarily engaged in sourcing and producing nuclear weapon materials, with many contractors helping. For example, the Battelle Memorial Institute, a nonprofit corporation, manages the Brookhaven National Laboratory, the Oak Ridge National Laboratory and others. The Departments of Homeland Security, Veterans Affairs, and Treasury, and agencies such as the FBI, the National Aeronautics and Space Administration and the National Oceanic and Atmospheric Administration also have cooperative relationships with the DoD. The Department of Justice, the U.S. Institute of Peace, and the National Endowment for Democracy are major participants in the humanitarian assistance aspect of "unconventional warfare," such as a current program to train the police in Nepal. In the 1950s and 60s an earlier U.S. technical assistance program was allegedly training the police in Vietnam.

FOREIGN MILITARY TRAINING

Particularly germane to the military mission is the State Department's program for Foreign Military Training. The 2019 report stated that "approximately 71,450 students from 157 countries participated in training, the total cost of which was approximately $904.7 million."[39] State also manages the Foreign Military Financing program that is implemented by the DoD. This provides grants for foreign countries to purchase weapons, and also supports training. Funding in FY 2021 was $3.8 billion.[40]

All weapons purchases (whether with grants, loans, or cash) by other nations are accompanied by training. A major element in State-DoD training, and crucial to networking with foreign military personnel as well as national security civilians is the International Military Education and Training (IMET) program that "introduces military and civilian participants to critical institutions and elements of U.S. democracy such as the judicial system, legislative oversight, free speech, equality issues, and commitment to human rights."[41] In FY 2019, the United States spent approximately $117.9 million for training students from 128 allied and partner nations.

International Military Education and Training is also provided to NATO member countries, but State reporting of this is not required.

Indeed, it leaves much out; within the unclassified report there are mentions without details of "Support of Special Operations for Irregular Warfare" and "Training for Eastern European National Security Forces."

CONTRACTORS

There are about three times as many contract personnel as those serving in the DoD as service members or civilians. What do they do? Later chapters will illustrate their functions in the system. They are employed in food, clothing, transportation, base construction and maintenance, environmental remediation, armed security for truck convoys, guards (armed and ready to shoot if attacked), intelligence analysis, cybersecurity, recruiting foreign armies, training foreign armies, and piloting drones.[42] For example, Edward Snowden worked for National Security Agency contractor Booz Allen Hamilton, analyzing data gathered from telephone and internet information. A foreign contractor, the Australian corporation Cubic Global Defense provided planning, execution and field training support for Talisman Sabre 2017, the war games for Australian and U.S. troops.[43] Overseas contract workers are often recruited from the local operation area or are third country nationals; the pay and benefits are good, but they suffer more fatalities than do the troops.[44]

This book, based entirely on open-source data, cannot tell the whole story. However, publicly available information is sufficient to provide a cogent overview of the vast array of interests (often unintended) entangled with the DoD, and the penetration of militarism into aspects of life normally considered civilian. More information on these processes and the institutions involved will be presented in subsequent chapters.

NOTES

The appearance of U.S. Department of Defense (DoD) visual information does not imply or constitute DoD endorsement.

1   James Madison, "Political Observations," April 20, 1795, in *Letters and Other Writings of James Madison,* Volume IV (J.B. Lippincott & Co. ed., 1865), 491. https://reclaimdemocracy.org/madison_perpetual_war/

2   Allen C. Guelzo, "Factors that Influenced James Madison to Declare the War of 1812" from *The Lecture Series: A History of the United States,* 2nd edition. https://www.thegreatcoursesdaily.com/factors-that-influenced-james-madison-to-declare-the-war-of-1812/

3   "The Madison Administration," Boundless US History: Securing the Republic: 1800-1815, *Course Hero,* https://www.coursehero.com/study-guides/boundless-ushistory/the-madison-administration/.

4   The U.S. has ratified the Biological Weapons Convention, but implementation and verification have not been settled. Indeed, actual adherence is another issue. The U.S. has ratified the Chemical Weapons Convention, but: "Subject to the condition which relates to the Annex on Implementation and Verification, that no sample collected in the United States pursuant to the Convention will be transferred for analysis to any laboratory outside the territory of the United States." The U.S. has ratified the Conventional Weapons Convention covering landmines, booby traps, incendiary weapons, blinding laser weapons and clearance of explosive remnants of war, but not the Ottawa Convention on anti-personnel landmines. While 170 countries have ratified the Nuclear Test Ban Treaty, U.S., Israel, Iran and China have not. The U.S. has ratified the Nuclear Non Proliferation Treaty, but neither the U.S. nor any nuclear weapon nation has yet ratified the Prohibition of Nuclear Weapons that entered into force in 2021.

5   Charter of the United Nations, Chapter 1—Purposes and Principles, Articles 2(3) and 2(4), https://legal.un.org/repertory/art2.shtml.

6   International Criminal Court, https://www.icc-cpi.int/.

7   *Truman Doctrine,* President Harry S. Truman's address before a Joint Session of Congress, March 12, 1947 (The Avalon Project, Lillian Goldman Law Library, Yale Law School), http://avalon.law.yale.edu/20th_century/trudoc.asp.

8   See Introduction for an excerpt from Eisenhower's speech.

9   Jim Mattis, *Summary of the 2018 National Defense Strategy of The United States of America: Sharpening the American Military's Competitive Edge,* U.S. Department of Defense, https://dod.defense.gov/Portals/1/Documents/pubs/2018-National-Defense-Strategy-Summary.pdf.

10 Nick Turse, "More U.S. Commandos are Fighting Invisible Wars in the Middle East," *The Intercept,* September 25, 2019, https://theintercept.com/2019/09/25/special-operations-command-military-middle-east/.

11 Stephanie Savell, "United States Counterterrorism Operations, 2018–2020," Costs of War Project (Watson Institute for International and Public Affairs, Brown University, 2021), https://watson.brown.edu/costsofwar/files/cow/imce/papers/2021/US%20Counterterrorism%20Operations%202018-2020%2C%20Costs%20of%20War.pdf.

12 Joseph L. Votel, Charles T. Cleveland, Charles T. Connett, and Will Irwin, "Unconventional Warfare in the Gray Zone," *Joint Force Quarterly* 80 (1st Quarter, January 2016). https://ndupress.ndu.edu/JFQ/Joint-Force-Quarterly-80/Article/643108/unconventional-warfare-in-the-gray-zone/.

13 Nick Turse. "Uncovering the Military's Secret Military," *TomDispatch,* August 3, 2011, http://www.tomdispatch.com/post/175426/

14 "Direct Action Short-duration strikes and other small-scale offensive actions employing specialized military capabilities to seize, destroy, capture, exploit, recover, or damage designated targets. Military Information Support Operations (MISO) are planned to convey selected information and indicators to foreign audiences to influence their emotions, motives, objective reasoning, and ultimately the behavior of foreign governments, organizations, groups, and individuals in a manner favorable to the originator's objectives. Unconventional Warfare Actions to enable a resistance movement or insurgency to coerce, disrupt, or overthrow a

government or occupying power." *United States Special Operations Command,* About, https://www.socom.mil/about (accessed 2/20/2022).

15 *U.S. Department of Defense,* About, https://www.defense.gov/about/ (accessed 2/20/2022).

16 "U.S. Special Operations Forces (SOF): Background and Issues for Congress," *Congressional Research Service,* updated May 6, 2021, https://fas.org/sgp/crs/natsec/RS21048.pdf.

17 "National Guard Soldiers Help Schools with Teacher Shortage," *Learning English, Voice of America News,* February 21, 2022. https://learningenglish.voanews.com/a/national-guard-soldiers-help-schools-with-teacher-shortage/6448907.html.

18 "Department of Defense Civilian Employment Opportunities," Department of Defense General Military Information, updated 9/23/21, https://www.defense.gov/Help-Center/Article/Article/2742213/department-of-defense-civilian-employment-opportunities/.

19 "Join the Military," *USAGov,* https://www.usa.gov/military-colleges.

20 "Senior Military Colleges," *Veteran.com,* https://militarybenefits.info/senior-military-colleges/.

21 NATO Education and Training, https://www.act.nato.int/activities/education-and-training.

22 "Natick Soldier Systems Center (NSSC) In-depth Overview," *Military Installations,* U.S. Department of Defense. https://installations.militaryonesource.mil/in-depth-overview/natick-soldier-systems-center-nssc.

23 Jane Benson, "Army scientists develop pizza MREs, slated for assembly March 2018," *U.S. Army,* March 16, 2018, https://www.army.mil/article/202192/army_scientists_develop_pizza_mres_slated_for_assembly_march_2018.

24 Mallory Roussel, "Natick Soldiers and civilians needed for Army nutrition studies," *U.S. Army,* January 21, 2021, https://www.army.mil/article/242457/natick_soldiers_and_civilians_needed_for_army_nutrition_studies.

25 "DARPA Enlists Insects to Protect Agricultural Food Supply," *DARPA,* October 19, 2016, https://www.darpa.mil/news-events/2016-10-19.

26 AnnMarie Harvie, "New England District's Junior Ranger Programs Teach Environmental Stewardship," *U.S. Army,* May 2, 2018, https://www.army.mil/article/204669/new_england_districts_junior_ranger_programs_teach_environmental_stewardship.

27 "The U.S. Army Corps of Engineers: A Brief History," *U.S. Army Corps of Engineers.* https://www.usace.army.mil/About/History/Brief-History-of-the-Corps/Introduction/.

28 U.S. Army Corps of Engineers, "Explore USACE Career Opportunities," https://www.usace.army.mil/careers/.

29 U.S. Army Corps of Engineers, "Volunteer Opportunities and Park Attendant Contracts," https://workamper.com/femp/64521/index.html.

30 David Vergun, "DOD Civilians Deploy to Support Warfighters," *Department of Defense,* October 8, 2019, https://www.defense.gov/News/News-Stories/Article/Article/1984281/dod-civilians-deploy-to-support-warfighters/.

31 "Defense Logistics Agency" search return, *USAJobs.gov,* https://www.usajobs.gov/Search/Results?k=%22Defense%20Logistics%20Agency%22&p=1.

32 U.S. Army, Outreach and Community Relations: Asset Requests, https://www.army.mil/outreach/request.html#knights.

33 U.S. Department of Defense Help Center, https://www.defense.gov/Help-Center/listing/Category/16423/.

34 Jon Skolnik, "Hollywood and the Pentagon Are Cheating on the American Public," *Monthly Review,* July 3, 2020, https://mronline.org/2020/07/03/hollywood-and-the-pentagon-are-cheating-on-the-american-public/.

35 Department of Defense Office for Diversity, Equity, and Inclusion, "Civilian Personnel in the DoD," https://diversity.defense.gov/Portals/51/Documents/Resources/Docs/Civilian%20Employment/Civilian%20Employment.pdf.

36 Department of Defense, *Base Structure Report – Fiscal Year 2018 Baseline: A Summary of the Real Property Data,* https://www.acq.osd.mil/eie/Downloads/BSI/Base%20Structure%20Report%20FY18.pdf.

37 Joseph Gerson and Bruce Birchard (eds.), *The Sun Never Sets* (Boston: South End Press, 1991); Catherine Lutz (ed.), *The Bases of Empire* (New York: New York University Press, 2009); Nick Turse, *The Complex: How the Military Invades Our Everyday Lives* (New York: Metropolitan Books/Henry Holt, 2008); David Vine, *Island of Shame: The Secret History of the U.S. Military Base on Diego Garcia* (Princeton: Princeton University Press, 2009) and *Base Nation: How U.S. Military Bases Abroad Harm America and the World* (New York: Metropolitan Books/Henry Holt, 2015); Thomas Fazi and Enrico Parenti, *Standing Army* (Rome, Italy: Effendemfilm, 2010).

38 "Cultural Resources," *DENIX* (Dod Environment, Safety and Occupational Health Network and Information Exchange), https://www.denix.osd.mil/cr/home/ (accessed May 9, 2022).

39 U.S. Department of Defense and U.S. Department of State, *Foreign Military Training Report, Fiscal Years 2019 and 2020, Joint Report to Congress,* Vol. I, https://www.state.gov/wp-content/uploads/2021/08/Volume-I-508-Compliant.pdf.

40 Nooree Lee and Emma Merrill, "U.S. Foreign Military Sales Down Over Thirty Percent in FY 2021," *Inside Government Contracts,* Covington, February 7, 2022, https://www.insidegovernmentcontracts.com/2022/02/u-s-foreign-military-sales-down-over-thirty-percent-in-fy-2021/#page=1.

41 U.S. Department of Defense and U.S. Department of State, *Foreign Military Training Report, Fiscal Years 2019 and 2020, Joint Report to Congress,* Vol. I, https://www.state.gov/wp-content/uploads/2021/08/Volume-I-508-Compliant.pdf.

42 On September 16, 2007, employees of a private military company (Blackwater Security Consulting, since renamed Xe Services in 2009 and then Academi since 2011) shot at Iraqi civilians, killing 17 and injuring 20 in Nisour Square, Baghdad, while escorting a U.S. embassy convoy. The killings outraged Iraqis and strained relations between Iraq and the United States. In 2014, the four Blackwater employees were tried and convicted in U.S. federal court; one of murder, and the other three of manslaughter and firearms charges. *See* "Nisour Square Massacre," *Wikipedia,* https://en.wikipedia.org/wiki/Nisour_Square_massacre.

43 "Cubic Aids in Success of Talisman Sabre 2017," Bloomberg, *Business Wire,* August 2, 2017, https://www.bloomberg.com/press-releases/2017-08-02/cubic-aids-in-success-of-talisman-sabre-2017.

44 Pierre Bélanger and Alexander Arroyo, *Ecologies of Power: Countermapping the Logistical Landscapes and Military Geographies of the U.S. Department of Defense* (Cambridge, Mass.: MIT Press, 2016), 252.

CHAPTER TWO

BASES AND INSTALLATIONS

The Department of Defense Base Structure Report (2018 is the most recent available) lists all land owned or leased, and buildings. Some of these may be small facilities such as listening posts, armories, or recreation areas, but a good number of the U.S. sites are the size of cities, and bombing and training ranges cover vast areas of our land.

Area	Army	Navy	Air Force	Marine Corps	WHS	Total
United States	1,565	785	1,535	190	75	4,150
Territories	40	62	9	0	0	111
Overseas	202	123	166	23	0	514
DoD Total	1,807	970	1,710	213	75	4,775

Base Structure Report   Source: DoD[1]

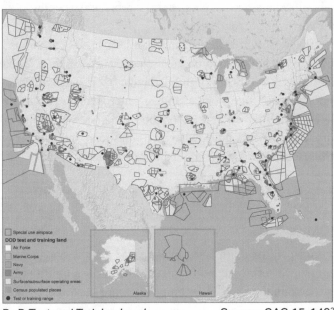

DoD Test and Training Land   Source: GAO 15-149[2]

Despite this considerable presence and the noisy skies that often signal it, there is little mention of the United States spatial occupation in discussions of the military industrial complex. There are excellent studies of U.S. bases in foreign countries and our territories, including books by Joseph Gerson and Bruce Birchard, Catherine Lutz, Nick Turse, and David Vine, as well as an excellent video, *Standing Army*.[3] Overseas bases will not be subjects of this work, although they are of economic importance in their localities, and provide U.S. corporations, especially construction companies, with monumental contracts.

While the media has paid some attention to global base relocation and expansions around the world, the massive military expansion under way within the U.S. has remained mostly under the radar. There is very little awareness of these efforts beyond the affected communities and regions. Every day there is news from around the world of the powerful struggles against U.S. occupation by the people of Jeju, Okinawa, Guam, and Hawai'i.

Less well known than the international fights are the many land base, air, and sea space expansions underway on and over the U.S. itself. Every expansion destroys fragile and important ecosystems, harms protected species, range animals, wildlife, and people.

There are three key elements of U.S. base expansions: 1) new and expanded land bases, airspace and seaspace; 2) base and military activities on public lands, tribal lands, culturally important indigenous sites; and 3) "encroachment" planning, the least publicized and understood category where the military basically dictates what activities can happen around military bases even on public and private land.[4]

Among the reasons for silence are economics and partnerships.

ECONOMIC HUBS

Reminiscent of company towns, bases are the economic hubs of their regions, fostering economic development in a multitude of ways. Military personnel and civilian employees are customers for car rentals, supermarkets, restaurants, entertainment, department stores—the whole suburban mall scene. These businesses, along with museums, recreational facilities, and historical sites, are featured on the bases' websites. Many personnel live off base, which benefits real estate sales and rentals, as well as hotel-motel chains, which offer housekeeping suites specifically for military families.

Base expansion and construction is a boon to local real estate interests. Frequent improvements to buildings, technical capacity, and measures against encroachments to bombing ranges also require expenditures, often massive, that benefit local as well as national and multinational corporations. For example, upgrades for cyber warfare at the Buckley Space Force Base in Aurora, Colorado have entailed many billions worth of contracts for weapons, technology, and construction companies. They claim:

> Team Buckley strives to be bold information technology investors who shape operations in, through and from cyber-space. Our emphasis is toward functioning and fighting as cyber warriors, defending our networks and core missions from attacks and preparing for offensive operations to execute when appropriate authorities direct.[5]

The five largest military bases in the world are in the U.S.: Fort Bragg, North Carolina (ten times the population of my city, Keene, New Hampshire); Fort Campbell, Kentucky; Fort Hood, Texas; Joint Base Lewis-McChord, Washington; and Fort Benning, Georgia.[6]

> Fort Bragg (population: 238,646, area: 163,000 acres) ... largest in the world. Fort Bragg serves 52,280 active duty soldiers, 12,624 reserve components and temporary duty students, 8,757 civilian employees, 3,516 contractors and 62,962 active duty family members. It is also home to 98,507 army retirees and family members.[7]

Anthropologist Catherine Lutz's fine portrait of Fayetteville, NC, where Fort Bragg is situated, describes the base's economic impact on real estate and "a virtual riot of shopping malls." In the wealthy neighborhoods of Fayetteville:

Here are the people who sell car insurance to soldiers, market houses at a steady clip sustained by station reassignments, and own the fast-food franchises that feed young soldiers' appetites. These neighborhoods house most of the medical professionals whose incomes rival any of their peers around the country, given the special market conditions of lush military medical funding and thin medical personnel supply.[8]

A company providing services to military personnel and their families, Millie, mentions that Fayetteville has been granted the title "All American City" by the National Civic League multiple times.[9]

Fort Bragg is the home of the United States Special Operations Command that includes the Special Warfare Training Group at the John F. Kennedy Special Warfare Center. Many of the locals see the Special Operations troops as a point of pride; they are, after all, "elite." Some neighboring citizens participate in their field exercise training or "war games" as "low-level source operatives."

Soldiers might contact a woman, for example, with the assignment to count the trucks driving by her house during a certain period. She would do this while hanging her laundry or mowing the lawn, trying not to draw the suspicions of opponent forces. In a "dead drop," or contactless exchange, she would pass on her information, perhaps in a black canister near the third tomato plant in her garden.[10]

While the many costs to Fayetteville that the base imposes include serious environmental damage, threats to endangered species such as the red-cockaded woodpecker, and loss of tax money to the city due to federal tax-exempt land and PX sales, to compensate for lost tax funds the DoD Office of Local Defense Community Cooperation provides grants to help "towns, cities, and states plan and carry out a future that is both sustainable and in alignment with the military mission."[11]

The Construction program enables states and communities to undertake necessary investments in public services and infrastructure to support the readiness and lethality of installations, as well as to provide safe places for services members and their families to live, work, and play.[12]

One grant for $985K enabled the city of Killeen, adjacent to Fort Hood, to create a local land use decision tool to make sure that its civilian development plans were compatible with critical live fire, maneuver, and mechanized training.[13]

Bases may host war games with live ammunition and bombing ranges, for example, those at Nellis Air Force Base, Nevada.

Nevada Test and Training Range   Source: Wikimedia Commons[14]

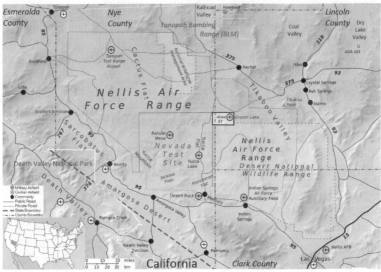

Federal Lands in Southern Nevada   Source: Wikimedia Commons[15]

CIVILIAN ENCROACHMENT

Readiness and Environmental Protection Integration Program (REPI)

The DoD's problem with civilian "encroachment" illustrates the military "spillover" not just into civilian land, but also into civilian institutions, governmental and non-governmental. The military has identified two threats to their ability to test, train, and operate: incompatible land uses and environmental laws protecting endangered species.

Such problems are to be resolved by the DoD Readiness and Environmental Protection Integration (REPI) Program.[16] Among the threatening encroachments are lights from residential and commercial development that reduce the effectiveness of night-vision training; restrictions imposed because of noise, dust and smoke of military activities; civilian use of the frequency spectrum; communication towers, wind turbines, highways, and energy transmission lines; construction or drones that enable observation into sensitive mission areas; foreign ownership of adjacent properties; acoustic monitoring in sensitive Navy areas; development in an explosive stand-off buffering area or accident potential zones; and land development that pushes endangered species onto military lands.

The REPI program employs "buffer partnerships" that include the DoD, private conservation groups (The Nature Conservancy is a major participant), universities, and state and local governments. Also involved, often as additional funders, are other federal departments: Homeland Security, Energy, Interior, Agriculture, and Commerce; and agencies, for example, the Agency for International Development (USAID) and the National Oceanic and Atmospheric Administration (NOAA). Partners may also include quasi-governmental organizations, for example, local economic development corporations; regional associations; and nonprofit organization coalitions, such as the Southeast Regional Partnership for Planning and Sustainability, the Western Regional Partnership, the California Defense Communities Alliance (which works with the Governor's Military Council), the Washington Military Alliance, and National Council of State Legislatures.

REPI regards these as "win-win partnerships," as these entities share DoD's cost of land or easements acquisition enabling the DoD to preserve compatible uses and natural habitats without interfering with bombing or other essential training exercises. These projects enable the military to exert an impressive influence over local development authorities, town councils, and adjacent landowners. "The DoD and its partners have protected over 757,000 acres at 115 REPI project locations in 35 states and territories through the end of FY 2020."[17]

Florida Sentinel Landscape   Source: DoD/U.S. Navy[18]

Here are a few examples of REPI projects. At Fort Benning, Georgia, home of the "Maneuver School of Excellence" (as well as the notorious School of the Americas, now renamed the Western Hemisphere Institute for Security Cooperation), live-fire and other training was threatened by threatened species and their habitats. Now the base and its partners are restoring habitat and offering contiguous land for buyers who would use the land for recreation. Among the partners are the Georgia Land Trust, The Conservation Fund, the Alabama Land Trust, and The Nature Conservancy (TNC).

Although actual conservation occurs, the projects incur entanglements, economic and reputational, between civilian conservation associations and the military. This can further silence the environmental movement, which rarely refers to the military's role in the devastation of the earth. They also provide a public image that environmental concerns are being addressed—even as ever widening territory comes under environmental threat.

Nationwide, TNC is likely the conservation organization with the greatest amount of DoD funding. The TNC grants for Fort Benning alone included (but were not limited to) one for $11,115,000, and another for $55,517,470.[19] Both were described as: "Assist State and local governments to mitigate or prevent incompatible civilian land use/activity that is likely to impair the continued operational utility of a Department of Defense (DoD) military installation." Another grant to TNC for $20m. for "Community Economic Adjustment Assistance For Compatible Use And Joint Land Use Studies," was awarded by the Fort Sam Houston, Texas, base and funded by the Army Environmental Command.[20]

Georgia also hosts the Townsend Bombing Range, with "airspace that spans 10 counties." The REPI partnership has protected an "ecologically sensitive area" and habitat to the "gopher tortoise and other rare species." Twenty thousand acres beneath the installation's low-altitude training airspace will remain undeveloped, ensuring encroachment protection. Partners include Ducks Unlimited, Georgia Ornithological Society, National Wild Turkey Federation, The Environmental Resources Network, and The Nature Conservancy.[21]

Washington State, very receptive to military activities despite the Hanford nuclear contamination area, has several REPI projects. One of them, at Joint Base Lewis-McChord on Puget Sound, is to eliminate the "threat" to live-fire exercises and other missions coming from efforts to protect imperiled species and incompatible development. The extensive area beyond its 91,000 acres became a designated "Sentinel Landscape," in a partnership headed by the Departments of Agriculture, Defense, and Interior to "align resources" to protect military testing "while benefiting ALL partners and landowners." The acquisition of buffer land will enable prairie habitat restoration, and easements on agricultural land will allow working farms, provided that their uses are compatible with the military mission. The partners for this project include Evergreen State College, Oregon Zoo, Sustainability in Prisons, The Nature Conservancy, Washington Veterans Conservation Corps, and Wolf Haven International.[22]

The REPI project in Maine serves the Navy's Survival, Evasion, Resistance and Escape School, which trains military personnel at high risk of capture. This training requires a harsh climate in an isolated wilderness to teach skills needed for long term land survival. The School also provides training in resistance to interrogation, indoctrination, and exploitation. The Navy is working with the Trust for Public Land to obtain conservation easements that will remove or prevent intruding commercial activities on adjacent land. Partners include Maine Audubon Society, Mountain Conservancy Collaborative, and Trout Unlimited.[23]

A REPI project at Marine Corps Base Camp Lejeune, North Carolina, aims to protect habitat for many endangered species, including the red-cockaded woodpecker. Camp Lejeune is "a massive installation that wraps around the New River tidal estuary and borders the Atlantic Ocean. The 156,000-acre facility has a mix of pine forests, calm river shores, and [eleven] miles of coastline available for amphibious and ground training."[24] Yet another of the DoD's environmental divisions, the Strategic Environmental Research and Development Program (SERDP), supports a Defense Coastal/Estuarine Research Program at Camp Lejeune. This is intended "to enhance and sustain its training and testing assets and to optimize its stewardship and conservation of natural resources through an ecosystem-based management approach."[25]

The Student Conservation Association participated in a ten-year research and monitoring program at Camp Lejeune with special concern for sea turtles, bald eagles, and brush clearing around red-cockaded woodpeckers. One grant, for the period July 4, 2016 to February 28, 2017, was for $152,000, awarded by the Navy's Office of Naval Research.[26] Another grant to the SCA in 2018, also from the Navy and at Camp Lejeune, was for $13m. This was for a program (now discontinued) "Troops to Teachers," training armed forces members for jobs in public schools.[27]

The Air Force also promotes conservation of endangered species. The Air Force Civil Engineer Center and U.S. Fish and Wildlife Service sponsor an annual event at Eglin Air Force Base in Florida for protection of sea turtles. When the turtles nest in May, "The base invites the public for a couple of sea turtle hatchling releases, and the participants also tag adult turtles with acoustic and satellite tags to track which areas to avoid during gulf missions."[28]

At the Poinsett Electronic Combat Range in South Carolina, a biologist with the Civil Engineer Squadron oversees care of at-risk red-cockaded woodpeckers nesting on Air Force training grounds:

"The red-cockaded woodpecker is the only federally endangered species we have at Poinsett Range," said Ronald June, 20th CES chief of natural and cultural resources. "They are only indigenous to the southeastern United States. You won't find them anywhere else. They're endangered because they're the only woodpecker that makes their cavity in a live tree and they sleep individually in the cavities. Most old-growth pine trees they prefer to live in are cut for timber, so you don't usually have old-growth." Because the range is managed by the Defense Department, the pine trees are protected and preserved for the endangered species. Due to the risk of the species disappearing, operations may need to be adjusted to keep the birds from harm on some military training grounds.[29]

Biologist looks for baby Red-cockaded Woodpeckers
Poinsett Electronic Combat Range in South Carolina.
Source: Dod/Air Force[30]

Legacy Resource Management Program

The DoD's Legacy Resource Management Program "assists DoD in protecting and enhancing resources while enabling military readiness."[31] The Department of Defense manages thousands of properties on the National Register of Historic Places. At the Naval Base Point Loma, California:

The Undersecretary of Defense Legacy Resource Management Program employs cultural resource managers who safeguard archaeological and historical sites on DoD lands in the U.S. and provide expertise for DoD departments and units operating around the world. Left: Prehistoric rock shelter, Fort Carson, Colorado. Right: Lewisburg Furnace, Fort Drum, NY. Source: DoD.

[T]he Post Exchange and Gymnasium Building 158, [is] a premier historic structure. Contractors, historic buildings architects, design managers and construction managers worked closely with the Cultural Resources Management program staff to retain the historic building's character and features while providing a modern workspace for the new occupant, Naval Base Point Loma's Security Department.[32]

At Patrick Air Force Base, Florida, the program led "six archaeological surveys, . . . [that] paved the way for the use of lands for the development of critical defense and launch programs."[33]

The DoD's many environmental agencies and programs are listed in its Environment, Safety, and Occupational Health Network and Information Exchange (DENIX).[34] Each branch of the military has its own programs, although these are networked in various ways, often involving participation of other government departments and civilians as contractors, partners, or volunteers.

TOXIC OVERSPILL

Encroachment can go both ways. The military literally overspills into civilian areas in many destructive ways:

U.S. military sites, which total more than 50 million acres, are among the most insidious and dangerous Pentagon legacies. They are strewn with toxic bomb fragments, unexploded munitions, buried hazardous waste, fuel dumps, open pits filled with debris, burn piles and yes, rocket fuel.[35]

There is no room here to encompass in full the environmental impact on land, water, air and outer space. A few examples will suffice to show how destruction becomes a distraction, and remediation a vast industry in itself.

The pollution of aquifers and surface water has long been a problem at the vast number of Superfund sites that are military bases and weapons production areas. Otis Air Force Base on Cape Cod (22,000 acres) contaminated the aquifer that provides drinking water for 200,000 year-round and 500,000 seasonal residents of Cape Cod. Superfund cleanup began in the 1990s, and now the Environmental Protection Agency brags about it:

> As of December 2015, the total groundwater extraction and treatment rate is 10.8 million gallons per day requiring 8,933 MW hours per year of electricity, all of which is produced by the wind turbines. Otis's cleanup groundwater program is unique because the treatment systems are all powered by renewable energy.[36]

At many other bases, new contaminents are being discovered and those affected are being informed. At Camp Lejeune, NC, the adjacent civilian areas, military personnel, their families, and base workers were subject to water contaminated with industrial solvents, benzene, Trichloroethylene (TCE). Perchloroethylene (PCE), Vinyl chloride, and other chemicals. Widespread contamination, on-base and off-base, by PFAS [Perfluorooctane Sulfonate (PFOS) and Perfluorooctanoic Acid (PFOA)]. On sites throughout the country has now been acknowledged by the DoD.

> Nearly 700 military installations have had a known or suspected release of PFAS—chemicals found in firefighting foam that can have adverse effects on human health. DOD is

in the early phases of environmental investigations at these locations. DOD has also acted in some cases to address PFAS-contaminated drinking water, such as by providing bottled water and installing treatment systems.[37]

The Government Accountability Office report of June 2021 included this graphic on the progress:[38]

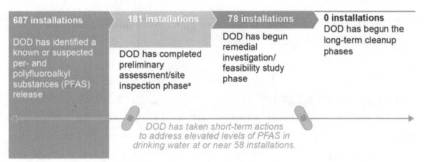

687 installations	181 installations	78 installations	0 installations
DOD has identified a known or suspected per- and polyfluoroalkyl substances (PFAS) release	DOD has completed preliminary assessment/site inspection phase*	DOD has begun remedial investigation/ feasibility study phase	DOD has begun the long-term cleanup phases

DOD has taken short-term actions to address elevated levels of PFAS in drinking water at or near 58 installations.

Progress on PFAS remediation as of June 2021   Source: GAO 21-421

Environmental Security Technology Certification Program (ESTCP)

PFAS has contaminated the seafood in waters near the bases, as the toxic foams seep into the ground and surface water. The DoD is seeking alternative less-toxic chemicals. Another of the military's environmental programs, the Environmental Security Technology Certification Program (ESTCP) works to find "cost-effective technologies and methods that address DoD's high-priority environmental requirements." Proposals are sought from government, academia, and industry. In December 2021, the ESTCP announced:

Mr. Jerry Back and his team from Jensen Hughes and the Naval Research Laboratory set out to identify an environmentally acceptable, PFAS-free firefighting formulation that met the performance of the legacy fire suppression foam. Through their efforts on this project, Mr. Jerry Back and his team have been awarded the 2021 ESTCP Project of the Year for the Weapons Systems and Platforms Program Area.[39]

The U.S. military is the largest consumer of fossil fuels in the world, with the resultant depletion of resources and carbon emissions. The Navy researches better practices for sustainability:

The Navy's John C. Stennis Strike Group, which consists of an aircraft carrier and supporting vessels such as cruisers and destroyers, began using beef tallow provided by Midwest farmers mixed with marine diesel fuel to power all of its ships except the carrier, which is nuclear powered. The project was completed in 2016 and the strike group was dubbed the Great Green Fleet.[40]

The Navy claims it is the world's leader in research on marine mammals. Its investigation includes "tagging, so that their movements can be tracked, followed by exposure to various acoustic stimuli, to observe the behavioral responses of tagged animals."[41] Many highly respected universities and conservation organizations participate in this research. However, until "proof" of harm is determined, if ever, harmful activities continue and threats to endangered species are intensified.

The Navy also collaborates with over 30 universities and institutions, with private industry, conservation agencies, independent researchers, and other world navies in developing and sharing information about the ocean, the species in it, and the potential effects of human activities. Some of the universities, institutions, and companies in which the Navy collaborates include the following:

• Bahamas Marine Mammal Research Organization • Stanford University • Boston University • NOAA Southwest Fisheries Science Center • Cascadia Research Collective • NOAA National Marine Mammal Lab • Cornell University • Oregon State University • Duke University • Texas A&M University • Elizabeth City State University • University of California Davis • Marine Acoustics Inc. • University of Maryland • Marine Mammal Research Consultants • University of Queensland • Mount Sinai Medical College • University of Southern Mississippi • New England Aquarium • University of St. Andrews • Scripps Institution of Oceanography • Woods Hole Oceanographic Institution • University of California Santa Cruz • Norwegian Navy • University of Aberdeen • Netherlands Navy • University of California San Diego • Royal Canadian Navy • University of Hawaii • Royal Navy[42]

LAND AND AIR INCURSIONS

Land use and overflights by the Air Force have been major irritants to neighboring and underlying civilians. The Kirtland Air Force Base in New Mexico uses the Cibola National Forest for Special Warfare training and also Osprey flights, claiming that they must train under the difficult flying conditions found there. In 2021, the Air Force obtained a permit to use the forest until 2041. It took 10 years for this process because of public opposition and environmental assessments, but it won. Logan Glasenapp, a staff attorney for New Mexico Wild, had said: "At the end of the day, in the back of our minds is a concern that our public lands may start to resemble war zones."[43]

Arian Pregenzer, a retired physicist living near the training sites who had worked at Sandia National Laboratories, said:

> I worked with the military. I have a lot of respect for them. But they need to be questioned. And they need to be held to account. Why can't you train at Kirtland? or White Sands? We have 5,000 square miles of military land in New Mexico, why can't they do it there?[44]

Patricia Johnson, a spokeswoman for Cibola National Forest replied:

> The U.S. Department of Agriculture and the Department of Defense have entered agreements that allow for such military training on national forest lands. National Forests are managed for multiple uses. To sustain mission readiness, the military needs to train under a variety of conditions and landscapes. Desert, mountainous and forested terrain are all found within the Cibola National Forest and National Grasslands.[45]

The Air Force commander stated that they would operate under restrictions, mitigate noise as much as possible, avoid any known golden eagle nesting sites, and not intentionally fly low over livestock, wildlife or dwellings.

Urban areas are also profoundly disturbed by the noise and environmental effects of overflights. In Burlington, Vermont, filmmakers Patrick McCormack and Duane Peterson produced a short documentary, "Jet Line: Voices from the Flightpath," with recordings of residents' reaction to F-35 jets.[46] These are now stationed in Burlington and are regularly noise-bombarding the citizens. "I have been getting recordings as high as 125 decibels. One, two, three, four, five jets one after another, severely shaking my house and rattling the windows," one resident said.[47]

Federal lands have been used for testing nuclear weapons, nuclear and chemical waste dumps, and bombing.

> In fact, much of what is today U.S. military land was, at some time, taken from Native peoples, sometimes at gunpoint, sometimes in the wake of massacres or forced marches, sometimes through starvation, and sometimes through pen and paper—broken treaties, acts of Congress or state legislatures, or by presidential authority by the "Great White Father" himself.[48]

The lands, including large areas of Alaska and Hawaii, have likely irremediable toxic contamination, and the adjacent surviving Native communities continue to suffer severe health problems and degradation of their environments.

> [In] 1951 the U.S. started nuclear weapons testing on Western Shoshone territory, at the Nevada Proving Grounds (now known as the Nevada National Security Site). The Shoshone can now lay claim to be the most nuclear-bombed nation on the planet.[49]

These encroachments generate much protest from the affected populations. The civilians and many organizations supporting their efforts must expend all their time and resources in attempting to regain their health, land, and sanity. They ask that the military stop the nuisance, clean up the toxins, and suggest that they "do their testing and training somewhere else." The military responds to these citizen protests with assurances that it will change, remediate, and engage military scientists, industry, and academics in research for less invasive ways to pursue its goals. The civilians who have been encroached are left with little time and energy for asking that the military mission itself be changed, and they face considerable social pressure against making such a demand.

The DoD uses the carrot and the commanding influence of military power. It emphasizes its need for natural landscapes for realistic training, its wish to avoid displacing or accidently bombing locals, and its help in protecting endangered species. However, it does not want environmental restrictions to constrain its activities. When the military wants more land, airspace, and ocean clearance, it will make concessions. Their environmental accommodations entail partnerships with governments, private organizations, businesses, and universities, which thereby acquire benefits from association with the DoD. In addition to economic payoffs from the giant federal budget, the projects do get some mitigation accomplished, in contrast to the democratic process which is often slow and uncertain.

Cleanup of military contamination is in many cases nearly impossible, yet this has generated a lucrative industry in itself, involving partnerships among the DoD, Environmental Protection Agency, state governments, and private industries specializing in remediation. Economic benefits also occur as the cleanup, inspection, and administrative personnel at military sites are customers for local motels, restaurants, entertainment and shopping malls. Billions have already been spent on toxic remediation at bases, and the Government Accountability Office has repeatedly warned that much more must be spent to deal with emerging contaminants.

MILITARY-RELATED RECREATION

Closed bases and those partially remediated may host "industry parks." In addition, some closed installations and even operating ones have decided that the way to win friends and influence people is to provide recreation, sports, and fun. Public hunting, fishing, and trapping is allowed on about 50 bases, "to support the sustainable multipurpose use of the resources."[50]

Many bases allow civilians with no military affiliation to hunt on them. Some do not. Fort Benning, Georgia, for example, is only open to military retirees, DOD employees, and military

ID cardholders and their dependents. Yet, if you read the regulations closely, you'll find you can hunt Fort Benning as a civilian if you're sponsored by someone from one of the approved groups.[51]

New Boston Space Force Station, New Hampshire, is a former Air Force bombing range and a superfund site. Now it is a more compact remote tracking station. The Air Force has determined that it has been cleaned up and currently offers much of its 2,600 acres for camping and recreational activities for those with a military connection. It has 50 campsites, four ponds, and equipment rental including skis, snowboards, poles, boots, snowmobiles, popup trailers, kayaks, canoes, boats, and bouncy castles.[52]

The Manhattan Project National Historical Park gives visitors the opportunity to see where atomic weapons were developed during World War II. It is managed by the National Park Service and the Department of Energy. It exists at three sites: Los Alamos, New Mexico; Hanford, Washington, site of the nuclear reactor that produced the material for the first atomic test; and Oak Ridge National Laboratory, Tennessee.

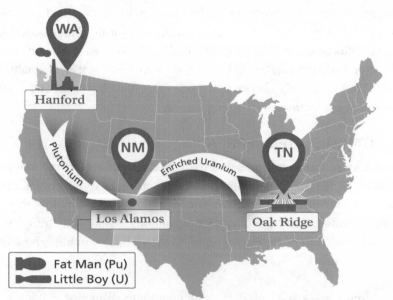

Manhattan Project National Historic Park   Source: National Park Service[53]

The Hanford park normally offers tours that include a 45-minute bus ride from the Visitor's Center in Richland, Washington, to the B Reactor. "The most toxic and voluminous nuclear waste in the U.S.—208 million liters—sits in decaying underground tanks at the Hanford Site . . . in southeastern Washington State."[54] It may be too dangerous to remediate. Its location in Washington State along the Columbia River was chosen by the Manhattan Project because of the abundance of cooling river water and hydroelectricity, thanks to the New Deal project celebrated in Woody Guthrie's songs.[55]

Workers at the Hanford Site constructed and operated the world's first nuclear production reactors that produced the plutonium used in the Trinity Test and in the atomic bomb dropped on Nagasaki, Japan, on August 9, 1945.[56]

As of January 2022, Oak Ridge and Hanford tours are temporarily unavailable due to the pandemic. Nevertheless, one can download Junior Ranger booklets, do the exercises, and "Mail your book to Manhattan Project National Historical Park, 2000 Logston Blvd. Richland, WA 99354 for a ranger review and to receive a badge or a patch."[57]

OTHER NUCLEAR SPINOFFS

Oak Ridge National Laboratory (ORNL)

Oak Ridge National Laboratory (ORNL) continues research and development on nuclear materials and engineering, robotics, aircraft design, and other military requirements. It has also become a general advanced technology laboratory, providing solutions for private industry and governments. A major involvement into the civilian world is its Urban Dynamics Institute, which has developed a sensor network and web tool for city planning. The tool, UrbanSense, uses information from virtual and physical sensors to capture and display people's minute-by-minute activity on computers. Some of the sources used are monitors of traffic flow and air quality. "Other data sources include online public data sets such as AirNow.gov and self-reported data from social media, such as Facebook 'check-ins' or Twitter posts."[58]

One ORNL project in 2021 studied "Impacts of the Morphology of New Neighborhoods on Microclimate and Building Energy Use." It used a Chicago neighborhood to determine how changes in urban design can lower building energy use and climate effects.[59]

Chicago Neighborhood   Source: U.S. Department of Energy[60]

The Laboratory's work has been appreciated:

> Researchers from Oak Ridge National Laboratory mapped and quantified hydrological changes throughout the country due to urban development, energy production and other human factors and won a prestigious award for their efforts. The team's analysis was published in the Proceedings of the National Academy of Sciences and received the 2021 Sustainability Science Award from the Ecological Society of America.[61]

Trinity Site National Historic Landmark

The Army, in a recent cooperative project, restored the McDonald Ranch House in the Trinity Site National Historic Landmark at White Sands Missile Range.

In July of 1945, Manhattan Project scientists used the ranch house to assemble the plutonium hemispheres of the atomic bomb. Scientists transferred the plutonium core to Ground Zero, approximately 2 miles northwest, where it was placed in the implosion device, referred to as "The Gadget," and detonated on July 16, 1945.[62]

McDonald Ranch House, White Sands Missile Range
Source: DoD/U.S. Army[63]

An archaeologist working with the Cooperative Ecosystem Studies Units (CESU) network administered by the U.S. Army Corps of Engineers contracted with a nonprofit organization, the Cornerstones Community Partnerships of Santa Fe, New Mexico. The restoration project was then undertaken by Cornerstones' archaeologists, architects, and artisans.

Projects like these serve the public relations efforts of the military. At the same time, they enable progressive organizations such as Cornerstones, with their experts and volunteers, to engage in work that aligns with their goals. Similarly, state and local governments, facing shrinking revenues because of economic changes as well as good old-fashioned parsimony, welcome the funding and activity emanating from the DoD budget. Local area businesses have new well-heeled customers for their goods and services. Who has the time or the inclination to think or talk about the lethality mission of the military, or the current "upgrading" of nuclear weapons?

Crew working on repair of perimeter wall   Source: U.S. Army[64]

NOTES

The appearance of U.S. Department of Defense (DoD) visual information does not imply or constitute DoD endorsement.

1   U.S. Department of Defense, *Base Structure Report – Fiscal Year 2018 Baseline: A Summary of the Real Property Inventory Data,* https://www.acq.osd.mil/eie/ Downloads/BSI/Base%20Structure%20Report%20FY18.pdf.
2   Legend with map: "For this report, we use the term 'major ranges' to describe both the Major Range and Test Facility Bases and Primary Training Ranges. The Major Range and Test Facility Bases encompass the largest, most-fully-equipped ranges whose primary mission is to provide test and evaluation capabilities to support the DOD acquisition system. The Primary Training Ranges are typically smaller, lesser-equipped ranges whose primary mission is to support the routine continuation training of combat units. Special use airspace consists of that airspace wherein activities must be confined because of their nature, or wherein limitations are imposed upon aircraft operations that are not a part of those activities, or both." https://www.gao.gov/assets/gao-15-149.pdf.
3   Joseph Gerson and Bruce Birchard (eds.), *The Sun Never Sets* (Boston: South End Press, 1991); Catherine Lutz (ed.), *The Bases of Empire* (New York: New York University Press, 2009); Nick Turse, *The Complex: How the Military Invades Our Everyday Lives* (New York: Metropolitan Books/Henry Holt, 2008); David Vine, *Island of Shame: The Secret History of the U.S. Military Base on Diego Garcia* (Princeton: Princeton University Press, 2009) and *Base Nation: How U.S. Military Bases Abroad Harm America and the World* (New York: Metropolitan Books/Henry Holt, 2015); (Video) Thomas Fazi and Enrico Parenti, *Standing Army* (Rome, Italy: Effendemfilm, 2010).
4   Carol Miller, "Connecting the Dots: US Military Expansionism – at Home and Around the World," *La Jicarita,* January 8, 2015, https://lajicarita.wordpress. com/2015/01/08/connecting-the-dots-us-military-expansionism-at-home-and- around-the-world/.

5 Buckley Space Force Base, https://www.buckley.spaceforce.mil/.
6 Everett Bledsoe, "Top 5 Largest Military Bases in the World by Population & Area," *The Soldiers Project,* June 2, 2022, https://www.thesoldiersproject.org/largest-military-bases-in-the-world/.
7 "The world's biggest military bases," *Army Technology,* June 3, 2019, http://www.army-technology.com/features/feature-largest-military-bases-world-united-states/.
8 Catherine Lutz, *Homefront* (Boston: Beacon Press, 2001), 6.
9 "Areas: Fayetteville," *Millie,* https://www.gomillie.com/areas/fayetteville/.
10 Catherine Lutz, 99.
11 U.S. Department of Defense, Introduction to OLDCC, Office of Local Defense Community Cooperation, https://oldcc.gov/introduction.
12 Ibid.
13 Ibid.
14 "Close Air Support training at the Nevada Test and Training Range" [image 9 of 10], photo by Tech. Sgt. Michael Holzworth, September 23, 2011, *Defense Visual Information Distribution Service,* https://www.dvidshub.net/image/468893/close-air-support-training-nevada-test-and-training-range.
15 Finlay McWalter, *"Federal Lands in Southern Nevada"* (topographic map), *Wikipedia,* https://en.wikipedia.org/wiki/Nevada_Test_and_Training_Range#/media/File:Wfm_area51_map_en.png [image licensed under the Creative Commons Attribution-Share Alike 3.0 Unported license].
16 U.S. Department of Defense, Readiness and Environmental Protection Integration (REPI), https://www.repi.mil/.
17 U.S. Department of Defense, Office of the Assistant Secretary of Defense for Sustainment Readiness and Environmental Protection Integration (REPI) Program, "2021 Report on REPI Program Outcomes and Benefits to Military Mission Capabilities," https://www.repi.mil/Portals/44/Documents/Metrics_Reports/2021_REPI_MetricsReport_FINAL_LOWRES_11JAN22v1.pdf
18 Illustration by Petty Officer 2nd Class Cody Hendrix, U.S. Navy, REPI, "New Sentinel Landscapes to Strengthen Military Readiness and Address Climate Change and Other Natural Resource Challenges" Feb. 15, 2022, https://www.repi.mil/Large-Landscapes/Sentinel-Landscapes/.
19 Award Profile Grant Summary for Department of Defense (DOD) award to The Nature Conservancy (Feb. 1, 2007–Sept. 27, 2012), *USASpending.gov,* https://www.usaspending.gov/award/ASST_NON_W911SR0620007_2100.
20 Award Profile Grant Summary for Department of Defense (DOD) award to The Nature Conservancy (Sept. 29, 2015–Sept. 28, 2025), *USASpending.gov,* https://www.usaspending.gov/award/ASST_NON_W9124J1520005_2100.
21 U.S. Department of Defense, Readiness and Environmental Protection Integration Program, *2016 REPI Challenge Fact Sheet,* June 2016, https://www.repi.mil/Portals/44/Documents/REPI_Challenge/2016%20REPI%20Challenge_JUN16_FINAL.pdf.
22 U.S. Department of Defense, Readiness and Environmental Protection Integration Program, *Project Profiles: Joint Base Lewis-McChord,* https://www.repi.mil/Portals/44/Documents/Buffer_Fact_Sheets/Joint%20Bases/JBLM.pdf.
23 U.S. Department of Defense, Readiness and Environmental Protection Integration Program, *State Fact Sheets: Maine,* https://www.repi.mil/Portals/44/Documents/State_Packages/Maine_ALLFacts.pdf.

24 "Marine Corps Base Camp Lejeune," *Millie,* https://www.gomillie.com/bases/mcb-camp-lejeune/.

25 "Conservation," SERDP-ESTCP, DoD's Environmnental Research Programs, https://www.serdp-estcp.org/Featured-Initiatives/Conservation.

26 Award Profile Grant Summary for Department of Defense (DOD) award to The Student Conservation Association, Inc. (July 4, 2016–Feb. 28, 2017), *USASpending.gov,* https://www.usaspending.gov/award/ASST_NON_N442551620069_9700.

27 Award Profile Grant Summary for Department of Defense (DOD) award to The Student Conservation Association, Inc. (Aug. 9, 2018–Sept. 22, 2019), *USASpending.gov,* https://www.usaspending.gov/award/ASST_NON_N624701827023_1700.

28 Courtney Strzelczyk, "Air Force environmental programs help endangered species thrive," Air Force Installation and Mission Support Center Public Affairs, August 1, 2020, https://www.af.mil/News/Article-Display/Article/2293342/air-force-environmental-programs-help-endangered-species-thrive/.

29 Destinee Sweeney, "20th CES protects endangered population," Shaw Air Force Base, June 4, 2018, https://www.shaw.af.mil/News/Article-Display/Article/1539642/20th-ces-protects-endangered-population/.

30 U.S. Department of Defense, July 28, 2020, https://media.defense.gov/2020/Jul/28/2002467216/-1/-1/0/180530-F-ZZ999-010.JPG.

31 DENIX (DoD Environment, Safety and Occupational Health Network and Information Exchange), *Department of Defense Legacy Resource Management Program,* https://denix.osd.mil/legacy/.

32 David Vergun, "DOD Announces 2021 Environmental Award Winners," April 22, 2021, *DOD News,* https://www.defense.gov/News/News-Stories/Article/Article/2579235/dod-announces-2021-environmental-award-winners/.

33 Ibid.

34 DENIX (DoD Environment, Safety and Occupational Health Network and Information Exchange), https://denix.osd.mil/.

35 Joshua Frank. "The Pentagon Is Poisoning Your Drinking Water." *Counterpunch,* August 25, 2017, https://www.counterpunch.org/2017/08/25/the-pentagon-is-poisoning-your-drinking-water/.

36 United States Environmental Protection Agency (EPA), *Superfund Success Stories: EPA Region 1,* https://www.epa.gov/superfund/superfund-success-stories-epa-region-1.

37 U.S. Government Accountability Office (GAO), *Recommendations,* https://www.gao.gov/products/gao-21-421#summary_recommend.

38 U.S. Government Accountability Office (GAO), "Firefighting Foam Chemicals: DOD Is Investigating PFAS and Responding to Contamination, but Should Report More Cost Information," June 22, 2021, https://www.gao.gov/products/gao-21-421.

39 "Capabilities Assessment of Commercially Available PFAS-free Foams," SERDP-ESTCP, DoD's Environmnental Research Programs, December 14, 2021, https://www.serdp-estcp.org/News-and-Events/Blog.

40 David Vergun, "DOD Recognizes Importance of Environment to Readiness," U.S. Department of Defense, April 22, 2019, https://www.defense.gov/News/News-Stories/Article/Article/1817776/dod-recognizes-importance-of-environment-to-readiness/

41 Department of the Navy, *U.S. Navy Marine Mammal Research Program Overview,* February 5, 2010, https://www.navymarinespeciesmonitoring.us/files/7213/4629/1083/USNavyMarineMammalResearchOverview.pdf.

42 Ibid.

43 Ryan Boetel, "20-year deal expands Air Force training sites in New Mexico's Cibola National Forest," *Stars and Stripes,* June 2, 2021, https://www.stripes.com/branches/air_force/2021-06-02/20-year-deal-expands-Air-Force-training-sites-in-New-Mexicos-Cibola-National-Forest-1621668.html.

44 Ibid.

45 Ibid.

46 Duane Peterson III & Patrick McCormack, Jet Line:Voicemails from the Flight Path, digital film, 12 mins. (2021), https://jetlinefilm.com/.

47 May Nagusky, "'The sound of freedom?' Crowdsourced film examines impact of F-35s in Burlington," *The Vermont Cynic,* April 20, 2021, https://vtcynic.com/culture/arts/previews/the-sound-of-freedom-crowdsourced-film-examines-impact-of-f-35s-in-burlington/.

48 Winona LaDuke, "The Militarization of Native Lands," in Gar Smith (ed.), *The War and Environment Reader* (Charlottesville: Just World Books, 2017), 163.

49 "'After 900 nuclear tests on our land, US wants to ethnically cleanse us': meet the most bombed nation in the world," *RT,* January 8, 2022, https://www.rt.com/usa/543541-us-nuclear-tests-shoshone-nation/.

50 Michael Herne, "How to Find and Hunt Military Bases in the United States," Black Rifle Coffee Company *Free Range American,* April 28, 2021, https://freerangeamerican.us/hunt-military-bases/.

51 Contributor profile: "Michael Herne," Black Rifle Coffee Company *Free Range American,* https://freerangeamerican.us/michael-herne/.

52 Shriever Space Force Base, Force Support Squadron, *Air Force Outdoor Recreation* (ODR), https://www.50fss.com/outdoor-recreation/

53 National Park Service, Manhattan Project National Historical Park, https://www.nps.gov/mapr/planyourvisit/index.htm.

54 Valerie Brown, "Hanford Nuclear Waste Cleanup Plant May Be Too Dangerous," *Scientific American,* May 9, 2013, https://www.scientificamerican.com/article/hanford-nuclear-cleanup-problems/.

55 Woody Guthrie, *Columbia River Collection* (Cambridge, MA: Rounder Records, 1987).

56 National Park Service, Manhattan Project National Historical Park, Hanford Visitor Center, https://www.nps.gov/mapr/hanford.htm.

57 National Park Service, *Junior Ranger: Manhattan Project National Historical Project at Hanford, Washington,* April 24, 2021, https://www.nps.gov/mapr/learn/kidsyouth/upload/Jr_Ranger_Booklet_MAPR-Hanford_4-24-2021.pdf

58 Oak Ridge National Laboratory, "City of Oak Ridge partners on advanced urban planning tool," *ORNL Review,* October 5, 2018, https://www.ornl.gov/blog/ornl-review/city-oak-ridge-partners-advanced-urban-planning-tool.

59 Earth & Environmental Systems Modeling, "Impacts of the Morphology of New Neighborhoods on Microclimate and Building Energy Use," *EESM Research Highlights,* November 15, 2020, https://climatemodeling.science.energy.gov/research-highlights/impacts-morphology-new-neighborhoods-microclimate-and-building-energy-use.

60 Ibid.

61 Thomas Fraser, "Ecological Society of America honors Oak Ridge National Laboratory scientists for sustainability research," *Hellbender Press,* https:// hellbenderpress.org/news/ecological-society-of-america-honors-oak-ridge-national-laboratory-scientists-for-sustainability-research.

62 DoD, "White Sands Missile Range: McDonald Ranch House, Historic Landmark," *Cultural Resources Update* Vol. 15, No.1 (Spring 2019): 9, https://denix.osd.mil/cr/news/newsletters/sprint-2019/.

63 Ibid.

64 Ibid.

CHAPTER THREE

CONTRACTORS

WHY DOES THE GOVERNMENT CONTRACT OUT?

The government practice of contracting for goods and services that the government might itself provide has a long history. It enables the government to avoid having to produce the latest technology, or to keep specialized staff on the payroll when they are only occasionally required. However, on the other hand, this entails loss of workers' rights (e.g., free speech rights and civil service pay and protections), and the weakening of democratic control over the service or project.

Further, private contractors' safety measures may be weaker, as they were in nuclear weapon manufacturing since the Manhattan Project and still are. In 2007, the Government Accountability Office (GAO) warned: "in light of the long-standing safety problems at the laboratories, GAO and others have expressed concerns about the recent shift in NNSA's [National Nuclear Security Administration] oversight approach to rely more heavily on contractors' own safety management controls."[1] By 2015, the concerns were validated:

> Recent internal government reports obtained by the Center for Public Integrity have warned that workers at these [plutonium processing] plants have been handling nuclear materials sloppily, or have failed to monitor safety issues aggressively.
>
> Personnel at Savannah River, for example, came dangerously close to a lethal nuclear accident in January 2015, when the stirring mechanism for a tank that held plutonium solution failed. . . . A spokeswoman for the contractor running the Savannah River site said it is "dedicated to maintaining the highest possible safety and security standards."[2]

While advantages from private contracting are sought, the results may be mixed. It may allow businesses and service agencies to follow local standards, reflecting popular will and possibly enhancing both democracy and productivity. On the other hand, the standards may be discriminatory on religious or racial grounds. Nevertheless, exaggerated budgets and loose restrictions spread the wealth around, keeping many businesses and employees happy. Contracting thus has popular support and Congressional enthusiasm for budgetary authorization.

Rationality and sustainability concerns may also be diluted when government uses contractors or provides grants, a somewhat looser mechanism. For example, railroads were built in the U.S. by bestowing land grants on businesses agreeing to build them. Aside from the questionable use of land that was violently seized or fraudulently obtained from indigenous peoples, the result was a crazy quilt of a railroad system: parallel lines, short lines leading nowhere much, and incompatible gauges.

Another example of "letting George do it," rather than Uncle Sam is the government's work relief agencies of the 1930s U.S. New Deal, which promoted "production for use" projects, whereby resources and workers were to be used to produce goods that people needed.

> Yet these plans never came to fruition. Production-for-use projects . . . challenged the logic of production-for-profit, and businesses and industry rose up in protest. The problem was that in production-for-use projects, goods were produced under the aegis of the government, which made its decisions on the basis of people's needs instead of business's profits. Thus it exposed the inability of the existing economic system to provide necessary goods as well as jobs. And it raised ominous fears of government taking over whole sectors of the economy, leading to the system most feared by profit-oriented capitalists—socialism.[3]

While it may volubly protest it, the private enterprise system is nevertheless still unable to function without massive government intervention:

The U.S. economy, although long government supported, has been increasingly weakened by foreign competition, outsourcing, automation, consumer satiation, rustbelting, poverty, and demographic changes. A "mixed economy" then fills the breach. Public-private entities in the form of local economic development councils have been created because the "free enterprise dynamic system" can do "everything better" (so its advocates claim), except keep the economy going. Capitalism must be saved by massive national, state, and local government investment and intervention in education, research, health care, highways and other infrastructure, transportation, agriculture, urban planning, environmental remediation, social services, recreation, business incubators, prisons, weapons, and much else.[4]

Political scientist Rebecca Thorpe's research indicates that after WW II many rural and semirural areas became economically dependent on defense spending. Their Congressional representatives initiated local projects regardless of an absent or negative national security impact.[5] Historian Frank Kofsky has argued that the Cold War was significantly motivated by the California aerospace industry, because it feared a postwar depression.[6] While *The New York Times* reported that unlike many rustbelt cities, St. Cloud, MN "sustained its prosperity through a mix of the right investments, favorable geography and sheer serendipity,"[7] it did not mention the bevy of military contracts in the area, which is easily discovered with an internet search in a government database.[8]

MILITARY CONTRACTORS

Despite the efforts of more than 2 million active duty and reserve forces of the DoD, plus "more than 70% of the federal workforce [of about 2 million civilians] in defense and security agencies like the Department of Defense, the intelligence community agencies, and NASA,"[9] private contractors increasingly perform military work. The DoD reports that about 75% of its budget is paid to contractors.[10] The revolving door between the Pentagon and weapons firms, campaign contributions from contractor PACs, corporation lobbying, and organizations such as the

National Defense Industrial Association, help to insure that the pump is primed.

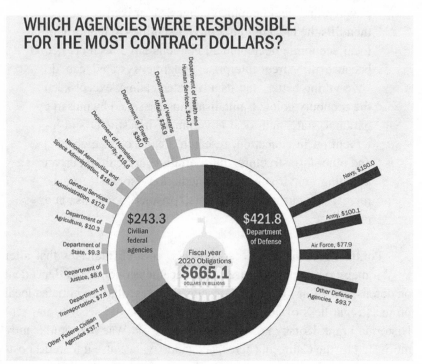

Federal Contracting 2020   Source: GAO

Military expenditures make for a perpetual motion Keynesian machine. While some of the products are meant to be destroyed after one use, the surviving ones can swiftly be declared obsolete, as the scientists and the corporations promise something more lethal. Furthermore, weapons are an important component of our manufacture exports, enabling us to import many of the things that people need that we no longer produce, as well as gadgets, fashion, and knick-knacks. The MIC advocates argue that since there is so little civilian manufacturing, our vast expenditure for weaponry is the only way to finance our technological advancement, which, they claim, will defend us against all the aggressive nations and terrorists that are out to get us, but also, in the bargain, lead to useful civilian spinoffs.

Production-for-use, rationality, and sustainability standards are often absent in federal government spending, such as the agricultural subsidies for monocrop, chemicalized, GMO commodity production, along with official government policies such as Popcorn Promotion.[11] Therefore, it is not surprising that usefulness is not a requirement in military contracts, even multi-billion-dollar ones, either.

One could well argue that most weapons are not only useless, but threats to the actual defense of the nation, the well-being of humans, and the sustainability of the environment—even before any use in war. However, "You can't fight City Hall," or the President, Congress, and Executive Departments. Even the top military themselves have questioned the need for and operability of some of our latest fantastically expensive armaments, such as the *U.S.S. Ford* aircraft carrier or the F-35 warplane. Congress has decided that they are useful, if not to fight or even function in any defense operation, at least to sustain local economies.

USS Gerald Ford Carrier   Source: DoD Navy

The military budget's economic payouts help to gain support, or silence, concerning our worldwide bases and "special operations," warfare conventional or unconventional, and the gradual militarization of everyday life. NATO's stimulation of our weapons exports contributes to the rationale for its prolonged life and expanded membership and operations. As our partners must have "interoperability," this requires the latest we provide in lethal equipment. After all: "To be effective when deployed together in operations and exercises, the forces of NATO member countries and their partners need to speak the same language and use the same technical standards."[12]

There will not be much discussion here of the weapons, or the corporations' campaign donations and lobbying in Congress, as these have been well described by William Hartung, in *Prophets of War,* and more recently in Christian Sorenson's *Understanding the War Industry,* as well as articles by Hartung and others in *TomDispatch* and *CounterPunch.* Instead, we will focus on those aspects of the contractor system that are less visible and those that promote the "creeping militarism" of our economy and culture.

As in most recent years, the top ten DoD contractors in 2020 were:

- Lockheed Martin
- Raytheon Technologies
- General Dynamics
- Boeing
- Northrop Grumman
- Huntington Ingalls
- Humana (a private health insurance company)
- BAE Systems
- L3Harris Technologies
- General Electric[13]

Their economic impact is multiplied many times by their subcontractors, their well-paid employees' spending, local tax receipts, and philanthropy. Thus, the *New Hampshire Business Review* reported that: "In New Hampshire, the F-35 program supports 55 suppliers—35 of which are small businesses—and over 900 direct jobs, much of them located at BAE Systems in Nashua. The F-35 program generates over $481 million in economic impact in the state"[14] In contrast to the widespread urban decay elsewhere in the U.S., *Money Magazine* has twice deemed Nashua the best place to live in the U.S. and is often on their 100 best places list.[15]

BAE is a British owned firm. Other foreign corporations that are frequently recipients of large DoD contracts include Leonardo (Italian) and Elbit (Israeli). However, U.S. firms are also multinational, engaged in manufacturing, building, selling their products, and sourcing parts throughout the world, while creating ties there to related industries, scientists, and charities. Many appear on the Stockholm International Peace Research Institute list of the 100 top arms traders.[16] For example:

Raytheon Technologies partners with Engineers Without Borders to support their work to build a better world through skills-based volunteerism and engineering projects that empower communities to meet their basic human needs. Our partnership supports projects globally—in countries like Tanzania, Nicaragua, Ecuador, and Nepal—and across the U.S.[17]

> Raytheon also gives grants to nonprofit organizations in Australia, Canada, Germany, Poland, Saudi Arabia, United Arab Emirates, and the United Kingdom. "We give preference to regional projects that serve the broader community in locations where we have major facilities."[18] Such a process creates a benevolent image and increases U.S. economic penetration of these countries, and their resultant concurrence with U.S. policy initiatives.

The military budget gets smooth sailing in Congress as contractors site their operations in every state and territory. Similarly, foreign support for U.S. worldwide military organizations and their operations, such as NATO, may be induced by international sourcing: "The Netherlands is one of nine countries that joined to help develop the F-35 Joint Strike Fighter, securing lucrative subcontracting deals for local companies from Lockheed Martin."[19]

CONSTRUCTION

Weapons production and sale is just one part of the picture; construction, technology, cybersecurity, policy analysis, and intelligence firms also secure huge contracts. In construction, Fluor, KBR, Bechtel, Jacobs, and Hensel Phelps are among the giants that work in the U.S. and abroad, building, repairing, and updating bases. Overseas, they employ U.S. and local workers, and often contract workers from a third country. During the endless wars in Iraq and Afghanistan, the extent of publicly listed contracts was likely understated, as researchers have discovered evidence of secret budgets. However, one of the reported 2009 contracts with Fluor (it was number 66 of the DoD top 100 contractors in 2020) was for $12.6b.[20]

Fluor simultaneously constructed and managed the expansion of various Forward Operating Bases (FOBs) in southern Afghanistan. This included the construction of bases to accommodate up to 17,000 to 20,000 U.S. military personnel. The urgent nature of the mission to expand the bases in front of a planned force deployment placed the project on the Army's critical path schedule. At peak operations, Fluor operated 76 Forward Operating Bases.[21]

In 2018 a division of Fluor received a $6.2 billion, 10-year contract for building nuclear reactors for the Navy.[22] An award, one of many, in 2012 for $123.8m to Hensel Phelps, a Virginia construction company (No. 51 on the DoD 2020 list), was to be performed in Aurora, Colorado; the description indicated "Commercial and Institutional Building Construction" and referenced a home-building firm, Mountainview Construction.[23] This was likely construction for the upgrading of Buckley Air Force base to the Space Force.

In 2005, Bechtel (22 on the DoD 2020 list) received a contract for $171m from the DoD's Defense Threat Reduction Agency, to be performed in the Republic of Georgia.[24] KEPA-TCI, a construction

Buckley Space Force Base   Source: Creative Commons

company and minority-owned purportedly *small* business in Wisconsin, has received more than $30m in contracts.[25]

Destruction as well as construction makes work for contractors. The Dome at Runit Island, Enewetak Atoll was built to contain radioactive waste from the vast nuclear bomb testing at the Marshall Islands. Efforts for decontaminating and containing have gone on for years, "but according to the Marshall Islands Nuclear Commission, more than 99 per cent of the waste has seeped into the atoll's lagoon."[26]

Runit Dome   Source: Wikimedia Commons[27]

INTELLIGENCE

Perhaps more surprisingly than the contracting out of construction and logistics is the military's contracting out of intelligence and cyber-security, despite the existence of 18 government intelligence agencies.[28] Information technology of all types has been fostered and supported by the DoD; Silicon Valley is an outgrowth of this command economy (with Microsoft No. 82 on the 100 top contractors of 2020). The corporate workforce may be graduates of the national security "feeder" institutions listed in Vice Magazine's 100 most militarized universities,[29] or graduates of national security programs at traditional colleges and universities. Many are ex-employees of government agencies, finding the atmosphere and the pay more rewarding at contractors. We had a glimpse into this world at Booz Allen Hamilton, "which is majority-owned by private equity firm Carlyle Group, [and] was thrust into the spotlight after [Edward] Snowden acknowledged being the source of news reports about National Security Agency data-collection programs."[30]

CIVILIAN BUSINESSES

Especially relevant to the argument here are the many "civilian" or formerly civilian businesses that are aided and often vitally sustained by contracts from the national security establishment, or those that are subcontractors and suppliers to the large contractors. Ball Corporation, still famous for jars, lids, and home canning products, is now number 88 on the Stockholm International Peace Research Institute (SIPRI) list of the world's top 100 arms-producing and military services companies.[31] Its website states:

> Ball instruments, sensors and spacecraft lead the industry
> in performance and value. Our advanced data services
> turn information into knowledge for the defense and in-
> telligence community, and our tactical systems support all
> branches of the U.S. Armed Forces with advanced C2ISR
> technologies.[32]

Honeywell (number 18 on SIPRI), FedEx, Microsoft, AT&T, Verizon, GlaxoSmithKline, and Martin's Point Health Care are in the top 100 of the DoD list of contractors. Martin's Point (number 91), now a nonprofit healthcare facility with branches throughout the Northeast serving military families, has a history as a military hospital:

> Our story began in 1858 with the opening of the
> Marine Hospital in Portland, Maine. The Marine Hospital
> was established to care for ill or injured merchant seamen

and coastal lighthouse keepers and their families. The facility also served as a Union hospital during the Civil War, and eventually came under the administration of the U.S. Public Health Service.[33]

Later it became a healthcare center serving the general community, and,

> continued caring for local military beneficiaries, including the Coast Guard, as a Uniformed Service Treatment Facility contracted through the Department of Defense.
> In 1993, Congress named Martin's Point one of six designated providers in the U.S. of the Uniformed Services Health Plan.[34]

No matter how small the amount of DoD funding, corporations, organizations, and their workers are not likely to protest the military mission or aid and abet those who do. Thus it is noteworthy that between 2008 and 2018, these publishers received DoD contracts: McGraw-Hill, Greenwood, Scholastic, Pearson, Houghton Mifflin, Harcourt, and Elsevier.

NEW HAMPSHIRE

New Hampshire is not widely thought of as a military state, despite its "Live Free or Die" state motto. The extent of its DoD business is barely visible even to many of its residents, as often the local press and governments are prone to referencing same by euphemisms like "high-tech," and "optics hub." The New Hampshire economy is largely based on health care, education, tourism, arts, entertainment, and various civilian enterprises. However, like much of New England, its traditional manufacturers long ago went South, and then abroad. Chairs, cloth and shoes are no longer mass-produced there, and wearing hats ain't what it used to be. There are artisans weaving and fine cabinetmakers woodworking, but their economic impact is minor. Today weapons manufacturers and their component suppliers form the major part of the manufacturing sector.

In 2020 these were the top ten DoD contractors in New Hampshire: BAE Systems (British), L3Harris Technologies, Cobham, Creare, SIG

Sauer (German), Safran Optics, L&C Protec, Red River Computer, Elbit Systems (Israeli), and Renco.[35] The extent of other types of military expenditures such as DoD personnel, National Guard subsidies, university contracts, ROTC and JROTC allotments, and base remediation is also economically significant, and contributes to the silence of anti-war protest—and often to cheering military endeavors.

Contractors and parts suppliers of all sizes are distributed far and wide in the state. Among the larger recipients in New Hampshire is Warwick Mills, now producing technical textiles such as those used in body armor; it was a cotton mill in 1888. Medium and small businesses also received stimulation from the DoD budget, such as Portsmouth Blind & Shade (window shades), Alan's of Boscawen (meals), Velcro (hook and loop material), Univex Corporation (fat analyzing kit), and Green Feet Enterprises (specialized mountain rescue training for Naval Special Operations Warfare). Childcare centers, heating oil companies, landscapers, carpenters, appliance dealers, and others get some of the pie.

In Cheshire County, New Hampshire, Timken (formerly MPB), a parts supplier, has the largest funding from the DoD. Other important contractors are Environmental Alternatives (nuclear decontamination), and C & S Wholesale Grocers (food and transport). Monadnock Lifetime Products (disposable double handcuffs), Filtrine (water filters), Stingray Optics (lenses), Abtech (laboratory equipment—one Navy contract was $324K) and Stellar Mechanical ($224K for earthquake repairs).

A rare survivor of our outsourced traditional manufactures, Whitney Brothers of Keene, New Hampshire, has been producing high quality children's wood furniture since 1904. In 2012 it was rejuvenated:

> It turns out the Army needs the Whitney Bros. cribs to replace old cribs at child care centers that do not comply with new safety standards established by the U.S. Consumer Product Safety Commission. The commission said all public childcare facilities will have to replace cribs with drop-down sides and others that failed to meet new, more stringent safety mandates by the end of this year.
>
> This contract is such good news for Whitney Brothers, [Melanie] Plenda [of the *New Hampshire*

Business Review] reports, the company will be adding 13 new jobs. That would increase the workforce by about a third. And, if the government needs any more cribs or other furniture, like changing tables, company management says it's prepared to add still more employees.

According to Plenda, that's not actually as far-fetched as it might sound. The DOD contract is "open source." That means "that any branch of the government that needs baby furniture or other wares made and sold by Whitney Bros. can buy from Whitney Bros." The Army contract lasts for at least three years for a total (so far) of about $866,000.[36]

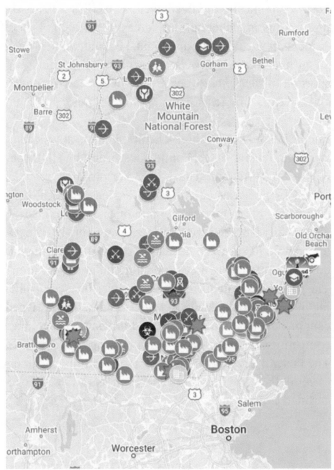

Interactive Map of MIC in New Hampshire[37]   Source: Joan Roelofs

As in the rest of the state, the nation, and worldwide, all kinds of businesses may receive a new lease on life. In 2018, *The New York Times* noted that Granite Industries of Vermont in Barre "makes 3,500 to 4,000 headstones a year for Arlington [National Cemetery]—a steady line of business in a town that has seen its stonework fortunes decline over time."[38] This may explain the vast silence regarding the trillions spent and millions dispatched, and why the headstones were needed.

PREFERENTIAL CONTRACTORS

The DoD has preferential provisions for contracts with small businesses owned by people who are socially disadvantaged (the DoD uses this term for people of color), veterans, service disabled veterans, women, or those economically disadvantaged, as well as for the AbilityOne Program and firms in "labor surplus" areas.[39] "In 2020, 45% of DoD's small business awards went to disadvantaged and women-owned businesses."[40] In many cases, owners need not be disadvantaged so long as a proportion of their employees are, or live in low-income areas. In addition to the DoD, any federal contracting has these provisions:

> Small businesses in high-unemployment, low-income areas can receive an economic boost from the HUBZone contracting program. The HUBZone program provides contracting assistance to small businesses located in economically distressed communities, referred to as Historically Underutilized Business Zones, or HUBZones, to promote job growth, capital investment and economic development in these areas, including Indian reservations. The program's benefits for HUBZone-certified companies include competitive and sole source contracting, a 10 percent price evaluation preference in full and open contract competitions, as well as subcontracting opportunities. The Federal government has a goal of awarding 3 percent of all dollars for Federal prime contracts to HUBZone-certified concerns.[41]

Hubzone Map, U.S. Small Business Administration

Contractors may be used without meeting location or competitive pricing standards. Silver Wolf Enterprises of Great Falls, Montana, an American Indian-owned business, provided "microwaves" (contract description, apparently kitchen equipment) to a DoD facility in Concord, New Hampshire. The preferential provisions not only bring a large proportion of businesses into the military supply system but create positive "public relations" for the DoD, especially appealing to human rights advocates addressing the situation of the related disadvantaged populations.

CORPORATE DIVERSITY

The top contractor corporations are not only major donors to minority organizations, often "partnering" with them, but also have extensive diversity and inclusion programs in their own operations. An example is L3Harris Technologies, a "global aerospace and defense technology" corporation, (number 9 in the U.S. DoD list and number 10 in the world SIPRI list). The company has an active Diversity Council and works to increase inclusion not only within its own workforce, but also in the local communities where it operates. It partners with national professional organizations of minorities and gives preference to suppliers with diverse employees.

L3Harris's latest report indicates that of its employees, 26% are people of color, 25% are women, 15% are veterans, and 8% are persons with disabilities. Women are 15% of the Board of Directors and 34% of executives; people of color are 23% of the Board and 18% of executives as well as 42% of new college grad hires. "In 2021, L3Harris was recognized as one of the Best Places to Work for Disability Inclusion and was included in the Disability Equality Index."[42]

They report that 7% of the executives are persons with disabilities. The company's many locations fly a rainbow flag in honor of Pride Month, and "they offer insights for leaders, HR [Human Resources] and team members into providing safe systems to support an employee's gender transition at work."[43]

For all its workers, L3Harris has an Employee Assistance Program that: "Provides confidential, 24/7 assistance, referrals and resources in a wide range of areas, including mental health and counseling; childcare and eldercare; adoption; home management; pet care; and financial and legal assistance."[44] They also offer paid time off, adoption assistance, parental leave, tutors for employees' children, and benefits for caregivers. "Dress for Your Day: Offers flexibility and discretion in choosing attire that corresponds to an individual's responsibilities and interactions for the workday."[45]

Is all this merely propaganda? Not likely. Evidence from the giant corporations' websites indicates that their boards and executives are diverse and do include women and people of color. For seven years, the CEO of Lockheed was a woman, Marillyn Hewson; Kathy J. Warden is Chairman, Chief Executive Officer and President of Northrop Grumman.

The lavish funding of contractors means not only profits for investors and high salaries for executives, but also good wages and benefits for all employees. These firms also provide ample time off for volunteering in public school and community projects, and matching the funds that workers donate to causes. Even the local or third country workers hired by contractors overseas are enticed by the wages, although the labor conditions are not always desirable.

There are various reasons for the progressive employment policies of the military industries, including the advantages they confer when dealing with weapons customers in our diverse world. These policies are enabled because, unlike much of our civilian industry, war is a growing part of the economy. This requires the hiring of additional people at all levels and permits the development of new divisions and programs. In addition, these corporations have had the foresight and resources to enthuse and train a diverse workforce from kindergarten on up, including via STEM programs in public schools, scholarships and internships for scientists and engineers, and partnerships with women and minority professional organizations. On February 24, 2021:

> Governor Ron DeSantis announced today that Lockheed Martin and CareerSource Florida have partnered to develop and refine a registered apprenticeship program. Lockheed Martin, one of the nation's leading global security and aerospace companies, has led the development of a regional workforce and education ecosystem and will model the program across its major regional operations in Florida and nationwide.[46]

The weapons firms have other channels for influencing progressive activists. Leading executives and board members serve on the boards of universities and nonprofit organizations, including those providing "technical assistance" to social justice and even peace organizations. Universities and nonprofits (including churches) receive excellent returns on their investments in military contractors.

LOGISTICS

Logistics, including guard duty, transportation, fuel, food, clothing, and janitorial services may not receive enormous funds as do the weapons makers, but they are very important to the companies involved.

Blackwater, a security and military training company, considered to be a private mercenary army, was contracted by the Department of State to provide guard and training services worldwide. Heavily armed, including with aircraft, and hiring additional local mercenaries, the company was involved in many shooting incidents and received serious publicity when "some of its contractors killed 17 civilians in Baghdad's Nisour Square in 2007. Four Blackwater guards were ultimately convicted for 14 of the killings, though former President Donald Trump pardoned them."[47]

Thereafter, the company instituted ethics training and changed its name several times. Now it is part of Constellis Holdings, a company merging Triple Canopy, Constellis Ltd., Strategic Social, Tidewater Global Services, National Strategic Protective Services, ACADEMI (formerly Blackwater) Training Center, and International Development Solutions. And again, "[Its] services within the global security market include delivering mission support, integrated security solutions, training and advisory services at home and abroad."[48]

Constellis Holdings' Board of Directors includes: Red McCombs (Chairman), former U.S. Attorney General John Ashcroft, former White House Chief Counsel Jack Quinn, Admiral Bobby Inman (Ret.), Russ Robinson, Jason DeYonker, Dean Bosacki and Triple Canopy co-founder Tom Katis.[49]

This company and those doing similar work have been contractors for the DoD, Department of State, CIA, and other government agencies.[50]

The U.S. military is the largest consumer of petro-
leum in the world. The Air Force ... expends over 85% of
its annual fuel budget to deliver fuel ... more than 75%
of the fuel is used for transporting and conveying it prior
to arrival at its final destination. ... In short, logistical operations prove the greatest consumer of the very resource
they supply; fuel demands only more and more fuel.[51]

FOOD SERVICES

No more GIs peeling potatoes:

Ameriqual Packaging in Evansville has been awarded a
$100 million contract to provide ready-to-eat meals to the
U.S. Department of Defense. The meals will be produced
for the U.S. Army, Navy, Air Force, Marine Corps and
federal civilian agencies.

SOPACKO of South Carolina and the Wornick Co.
in Cincinnati also received contracts totaling more than
$275 million. The individual pork-free/humanitarian
daily rations will be produced in Indiana, South Carolina
and Ohio, with an ordering period end date of November
1, 2026.[52]

Ameriqual, which claims to be the leading supplier of food to the
U.S. military, also feeds militaries around the globe and provides global
humanitarian and disaster relief rations.[53] Some examples of military
menus, known as Meal, Ready-to-Eat (MREs):

Menu #1 Chili with Beans, Cheese Spread, Cheddar, Plain
Crackers, Vegetable, Cornbread, Cheese Filled Crackers,
Pepperoni Pizza, Beverage Powder, Carbohydrate,
Fortified, Lemon Lime, Accessory Packet A, Spoon,
Flameless Ration Heater Bag, Hot Beverage, Paperboard
Sleeve

Menu #2 Beef, Shredded, in Barbecue Sauce, Black
Beans in a Seasoned Sauce, Cheese Spread, Cheddar,
with Jalapeno Peppers, Tortillas, Plain Oatmeal Cookie,

Plain Beverage Powder, Carbohydrate, Fortified, Orange
Barbecue Sauce, Accessory Packet C, Spoon, Flameless
Ration Heater Bag, Hot Beverage, Paperboard Sleeve,
Paperboard Insert Card[54]

The company's humanitarian rations are for:

feeding large populations of displaced persons or refu-
gees under emergency conditions. The HDR is similar in
concept to the Meal, Ready-to-Eat as it is composed of
ready-to-eat thermostabilized entrees and complementary
components and is packaged in materials structurally
similar to the MRE.... The components are designed to
provide a full day's sustenance to a moderately malnour-
ished individual. In order to provide the widest possible
acceptance from the variety of potential consumers with
diverse religious and dietary restrictions from around the
world, the HDR contains no animal products or animal
by-products, except that minimal amounts of dairy products are permitted.[55]

Investments in hogsheads may not have much of a future, but the
processed food companies are doing well in the stock indices. The military has had a historic role in pioneering food preservation techniques,
since it was very long ago that armies lived off the land they traversed.

CLOTHING

Propper claims to be the largest supplier of U.S. military uniforms.
Its website states:

We cut and sew our apparel and gear in our very own
9001-2008 ISO-Certified production facilities in Haiti
and Dominican Republic as well as sourcing and manufacturing through our global partners. Propper's Berry-
Compliant production facility in Puerto Rico handles
additional cutting and sewing.[56]

Small, medium and large clothing firms, some with part or all of the production process in the U.S., have contracts. One with vital support is Kaos Worldwide, which received a $1.5 million DoD contract in 2009 to supply sports bras.

According to the Berry Amendment, a U.S. law originating in 1941, all production for the government is supposed to be U.S. based, including the materials used. However, there are exceptions to the law, including to the size of the contract—under $250,000 is exempt—and a determination "that a sufficient quantity and satisfactory quality of items grown, reprocessed, reused, or produced in the United States cannot be acquired at U.S. market prices."[57]

U.S. factories still produce specialty textiles, like the Turtleskin of Warwick Mills, but ordinary cloth is not mass-produced here these days; it is likely that cloth for uniforms is sourced from other nations—not only the cloth, but fabrication. Burlington Fabrics, another major military supplier is headquartered in North Carolina, but it operates also in Mexico and China:

> Jiaxing Burlington Textile Co., Ltd (JBT) Voted as a model facility for the Jiaxing Economic Industrial Zone for its reduced waste water processing. Provides finished fabric for Performance Apparel, Medical/ Cleanroom, Apparel, Uniform, and Home Interior products. Supported by Burlington Labs in the U.S., JBT's high-tech lab and product development resources are dedicated to bringing our customers the best in cutting-edge technologies. Multiple investments in Eco-friendly processes.[58]

NONPROFIT ORGANIZATIONS

Our government is a major subsidizer of the "free enterprise" sector, and also a crucial support for the nonprofit sector. The DoD contracts with many nonprofits and thereby influences their staff, donors, clients, and volunteers. It is no surprise that the military outsources research to think tanks, weapons research laboratories, and information technology firms that have organized themselves as nonprofits. Some of these do a major proportion of their work for government, such as RAND and the Draper Laboratory, and are effectively part of the establishment, yet they are still technically nongovernmental organizations. Universities and think tanks will be discussed in Chapter 4 but let us note here in passing that the Massachusetts Institute of Technology is number 38 of all U.S. military contractors.

What is surprising is the vast range of charitable, environmental, health, professional associations and policy organizations associated with the MIC. For example, the DoD has partnerships with the Council on State Governments, a research and lobbying organization for the states that is itself an NGO (more on this in Chapter 6).

Disabled people can be usefully employed. The DoD has large contracts for janitorial services, landscaping, clothing, and furniture with Goodwill Industries, Lighthouse for the Blind, Northern New England Employment Services, Jewish Vocational Service and Community Workshop, and other nonprofit corporations employing disabled people, veterans, and people with chronic difficulty finding work. These form a significant part of the U.S. *citizen* low-income working class. Another sector of our low-income working class consists of *noncitizens,* therefore nonvoters, and they are rarely able to safely participate in any political activity, including antiwar.

As in the jobs programs of the Depression-era Works Progress Administration, contractors serve as administrators. Goodwill Industries consists of many separate corporations; some states have several, and the total contracts are in the billions. Its services provided to the military include records processing, Army combat pants, custodial, security, mowing, and recycling.

ENVIRONMENTAL ORGANIZATIONS

Of all the environmental organizations funded by the military, The Nature Conservancy (TNC) appears to receive the greatest funding via contracts and grants. The grants are the largest, and mainly serve to create buffer zones that mitigate encroachment from civilian activities onto bombing and other training ranges. (See discussion in Chapter 2). Two of the grants received by TNC for work at Fort Benning, Georgia, were for $11m and $56m; some mitigation at other bases run into the multimillions. Grants are also related to protection of oyster habitat, rare species, burrowing owls, and ground squirrels, and the monitoring of grasslands. TNC's contracts include projects related to the streaked horned lark, whiteface mitigation monitoring, ecosystem restoration course, water and the watershed, and invasive species control. TNC also receives substantial grants from USAID for overseas work.

Other environmental organizations with large contracts or grants are the Student Conservation Association, the National Audubon Society, and the Point Reyes Bird Observatory. Woods Hole Oceanographic Institute, Trout Unlimited, Ducks Unlimited, many zoos, and the U.S. Green Building Council are also employed or funded. The Monterey Bay Aquarium has received millions in contracts and grants. One of its contracts from the Defense Advanced Research Projects Agency (DARPA) was for Persistent Ocean Surveillance Support; DARPA also issued a grant for a Renewable At Sea-Power Program, a component of undersea warfare:

> Over the next twenty years, the proliferation of threats in the undersea environment will likely challenge the platform-centric model that the United States Navy uses to maintain dominance in Undersea Warfare (USW). Meanwhile, rapidly maturing technologies offer greater capabilities to potential adversaries around the world. Such a paradigm creates an imperative for the Navy to harness emerging technologies to maintain USW dominance amid a dynamic threat environment, while balancing cost, risk, and required performance.[59]

Cetacean research is heavily supported, often with collaborations that may be worldwide among businesses, nonprofits, universities, and DoD agencies. Grantees include the New England Aquarium (for assessing stress in whales), the University of St. Andrews, Scotland, and Kelp, a Netherlands organization (to study Cetacean Social Behavioral Response to Sonar).

HEALTH

Health care is one of the largest industries in the U.S., and here also the DoD has a significant role. This is a historic connection, as for many centuries the fatality rate from disease was greater than that from enemy attack. Military research led to developments vital to civilian medical care, such as tourniquets, antibiotics, ambulances, and prosthetics. Today in the age of robotic warfare, threats to troops and their families nevertheless loom large from mental health issues, suicide, homicide, addiction, and assault.

Humana, a for-profit health insurance corporation, is number 7 in the top ten of DoD contractors, outranking three major weapons companies. It provides enhanced care for service members, retirees, and veterans, working in cooperation with the Department of Veterans Affairs medical system.

Nonprofit contractors include most well-known hospitals, such as Massachusetts General Hospital, the Mayo Clinic, and medical research firms, notably the Battelle Memorial Institute. The latter is a massive nonprofit enterprise that undertakes, among many other services for the military, life sciences research, public health studies, and biosafety operations. "Battelle Memorial Institute is the world's largest nonprofit research and development organization, with over 20,000 employees at more than 100 locations globally. Based in Columbus, Ohio, Battelle is a 501(c)(3) charitable trust...."[60]

The American Red Cross with long military associations, the American Heart Association, and Martin's Point Health Care are among the contractors. Biotechnology research is funded in U.S. universities and institutes and worldwide, including Eastern and Western Europe, Israel, Southeast Asia, Africa, and South America. Reflecting today's concerns, the military contracts with the Rape, Abuse, and Incest National Network; and the Voices and Faces Project, "an award-winning non-profit storytelling initiative created to bring the names, faces, and testimonies of survivors of gender-based violence to the attention of the public."[61]

HUMAN RIGHTS

Contracts with human rights organizations include the Fair Labor Association (FLA), which absorbed the disruptive wave of activism on college campuses:

> Since 1999, the Fair Labor Association has helped im-
> prove the lives of millions of workers around the world. As
> a collaborative effort of socially responsible companies,
> colleges and universities, and civil society organizations,
> FLA creates lasting solutions to abusive labor practices
> by offering tools and resources to companies, delivering

training to factory workers and management, conducting due diligence through independent assessments, and advocating for greater accountability and transparency from companies, manufacturers, factories and others involved in global supply chains.[62]

Other contracted human rights nonprofits include Focus HOPE: "Recognizing the dignity and beauty of every person, we pledge intelligent and practical action to overcome racism, poverty, and injustice. And to build a metropolitan community where all people may live in freedom, harmony, trust and affection."[63] and Partners Achieving Success: "to support, promote and encourage community development that helps at-risk youth and parents through worthy community-based training programs that help those in need."[64]

EDUCATIONAL AND PROFESSIONAL ORGANIZATIONS

The DoD has contracts with the American Council on Education, American Association of State Colleges and Universities, Association of American Law Schools, and gives grants to the Institute of International Education. Its considerable ties to educational institutions of all types will be discussed in Chapter 4.

Among DoD contractors are the Society of Women Engineers, American Dental Assistants Association, Society of Hispanic Professionals, National Society of Black Engineers, American Indian Science and Engineering Society, Asian Pacific American Medical Student Association, National Black Law Students Association, American Association of Nurse Anesthetists, Society of Mexican-American Engineers. These are likely for scholarships, internships, recruitment, or booths at conferences, which not only present the most positive images of the military but can result in solid employment opportunities.

The obvious functions of the contract system are obtaining the goods and services necessary to defend the nation, cementing the ties with businesses and nonprofits in the U.S. and worldwide, and keeping the economy going. It does not take a rocket scientist to figure out more effective and ethical ways of accomplishing these objectives without having to use the military as an intermediary.

NOTES

The appearance of U.S. Department of Defense (DoD) visual information does not imply or constitute DoD endorsement.

1   U.S. Government Accountability Office, "Nuclear And Worker Safety: Actions Needed to Determine the Effectiveness of Safety Improvement Efforts at NNSA's Weapons Laboratories" (report no. GAO-08-73), November 28, 2007, https://www.gao.gov/assets/a268646.html.

2   Patrick Malone, "Key sites proposed for nuclear bomb production are plagued by safety problems," The Center for Public Integrity, May 1, 2018, https://publicintegrity.org/national-security/key-sites-proposed-for-nuclear-bomb-production-are-plagued-by-safety-problems/.

3   Nancy E. Rose, *Put to Work: The WPA and Public Employment in the Great Depression* (New York: Monthly Review Press, 2009), 57.

4   Joan Roelofs, "Military Keynesianism Marches On," *Counterpunch* (Oct. 3, 2019), https://www.counterpunch.org/2019/10/03/military-keynesianism-marches-on/.

5   Rebecca U. Thorpe, *The American Warfare State: The Domestic Politics of Military Spending* (Chicago: University of Chicago Press, 2014), 6.

6   Frank Kofsky, *Harry S. Truman and the War Scare of 1948: A Successful Campaign to Deceive the Nation* (New York: St. Martin's Press, 1993).

7   Eduardo Porter, "Lessons From Rust-Belt Cities That Kept Their Sheen," *The New York Times*, May 1, 2018, https://www.nytimes.com/2018/05/01/business/economy/rust-belt-cities.html.

8   Search by location or zip code + Department of Defense at https://www.usaspending.gov. The contract and grant data in this chapter and throughout the book are taken from this government database.

9   Fiona Hill, "Public service and the federal government," *Policy 2020*, Brookings, May 27, 2020, https://www.brookings.edu/policy2020/votervital/public-service-and-the-federal-government/.

10 U.S. Department of Defense, Office of Local Defense Community Cooperation, "DoD Releases Report on Defense Spending by State in Fiscal Year 2020," October 22, 2021, https://oldcc.gov/dod-releases-report-defense-spending-state-fiscal-year-2020.

11 U.S. Department of Agriculture, Agricultural Marketing Service, "Popcorn Board," https://www.ams.usda.gov/rules-regulations/research-promotion/popcorn. Potato chips are not neglected! They were included in the U.S. Code of Federal Regulations, Part 1207: Potato Research and Promotion Plan, https://www.ecfr.gov/current/title-7/part-1207. Among its provisions: "The establishment, issuance, effectuation and administration of appropriate programs or projects for the advertising and promotion of potatoes and potato products: *Provided, however,* That any such program or project shall be directed toward increasing the general demand for potatoes and potato products..."

12 North Atlantic Treaty Organization (NATO), "A common language for NATO and its partners," November 19-20, 2015 (last updated November 27, 2015), https://www.nato.int/cps/en/natohq/news_125041.htm.

13 "Top-100 Defense Contractors 2020," Forecast International's Aerospace Portal, *Aeroweb*, http://www.fi-aeroweb.com/Top-100-Defense-Contractors.html.

14 *New Hampshire Business Review*, September 21, 2017.

15 "Nashua Makes 2019 Money Magazine Best Places to Live!," *DowntownNashua. org,* September 16, 2019, https://downtownnashua.org/nashua-makes-2019-money-magazine-best-places-to-live/.

16 Alexandra Marksteiner, Lucie Béraud-Sudreau, Nan Tian, Diego Lopes da Silva and Alexandra Kuimova, "The SIPRI Top 100 Arms-producing and Military Service Companies," SIPRI Fact Sheet, Stockholm International Peace Research Institute, December 2021, https://sipri.org/sites/default/files/2021-12/fs_2112_top_100_2020.pdf.

17 Raytheon Technologies, "Strategic Partners," https://www.rtx.com/social-impact/corporate-responsibility/partners.

18 "Raytheon Grants," *Instrumentl,* https://www.instrumentl.com/grants/raytheon-grants.

19 Nicola Clark, "Dutch Pick F-35 Jets to Expand Aging Fleet," *The New York Times,* September 18, 2013, http://www.nytimes.com/2013/09/18/business/global/dutch-choose-f-35-fighter-jets-but-fewer-of-them.html.

20 Award Profile Contract Summary for Department of Defense (DOD) award to Fluor Intercontinental Incorporated (July 7, 2009–June 30, 2022), *USAspending. gov,* https://www.usaspending.gov/award/CONT_AWD_0005_9700_W52P1J07D0008_9700.

21 "U.S. Army Logistics Civil Augmentation Program (LOGCAP IV)," Fluor projects, https://www.fluor.com/projects/contingency-operations-logistics-construction.

22 Award Profile Contract Summary for Department of Defense (DOD) award to Fluor Marine Propulsion, LLC (July 12, 2018–September 30, 2028), *USASpending. gov,* https://www.usaspending.gov/award/CONT_AWD_N0002418C2130_9700_-NONE-_-NONE-.

23 Award Profile Contract Summary for Department of Defense (DOD) award to Hensel Phelps Construction Co. (September 26, 2012–June 7, 2019), *USASpending.gov,* https://www.usaspending.gov/award/CONT_AWD_W912DR12C0019_9700_-NONE-_-NONE-.

24 Award Profile Contract Summary for Department of Defense (DOD) award to Bechtel National, Inc. (June 7, 2005–October 31, 2010), *USASpending.gov.,* https://www.usaspending.gov/award/CONT_AWD_0014_9700_DTRA0101D0011_9700.

25 Kepa-Tci JV LLC vendor profile, *GovTribe.com,* https://govtribe.com/vendors/kepa-tci-jv-llc-6vch0.

26 Mackenzie Smith, "Leaking nuclear waste dome: Marshalls consider legal action," *RNZ,* October 29, 2019, https://www.rnz.co.nz/international/pacific-news/402002/leaking-nuclear-waste-dome-marshalls-consider-legal-action.

27 U.S. Defense Special Weapons Agency, public domain, via Wikimedia Commons https://commons.wikimedia.org/wiki/File:Runit_Dome_001.jpg.

28 The U.S. Intelligence Community is composed of the following 18 organizations: Two independent agencies—the Office of the Director of National Intelligence (ODNI) and the Central Intelligence Agency (CIA); Nine Department of Defense elements—the Defense Intelligence Agency (DIA), the National Security Agency (NSA), the National Geospatial-Intelligence Agency (NGA), the National Reconnaissance Office (NRO), and intelligence elements of the five DoD services; the Army, Navy, Marine Corps, Air Force, and Space Force.
Seven elements of other departments and agencies—the Department of Energy's Office of Intelligence and Counter-Intelligence; the Department of Homeland Security's Office of Intelligence and Analysis and U.S. Coast Guard Intelligence;

the Department of Justice's Federal Bureau of Investigation and the Drug Enforcement Agency's Office of National Security Intelligence; the Department of State's Bureau of Intelligence and Research; and the Department of the Treasury's Office of Intelligence and Analysis ["Members of the IC," Office of the Director of National Intelligence, https://www.dni.gov/index.php/what-we-do/members-of-the-ic].

29 William M. Arkin and Alexa O'Brien, "The Most Militarized Universities in America: A VICE News Investigation," *VICE News,* November 6, 2015, https://www.vice.com/en/article/j59g5b/the-most-militarized-universities-in-america-a-vice-news-investigation

30 Marjorie Censer, "Booz CEO: Snowden 'was not a Booz Allen person,'" *The Washington Post,* July 31, 2013, https://www.washingtonpost.com/business/capitalbusiness/booz-ceo-snowden-was-not-a-booz-allen-person/2013/07/31/a349b51a-f9f6-11e2-8752-b41d7ed1f685_story.html.

31 Alexandra Marksteiner et al., SIPRI Fact Sheet, https://sipri.org/sites/default/files/2021-12/fs_2112_top_100_2020.pdf.

32 Ball Corporation, "About Aerospace," https://www.ball.com/aerospace/about-aerospace.

33 Martin's Point Health Care, "Our History," https://martinspoint.org/meet-martins-point/about-martins-point/history.

34 Ibid.

35 U.S. Department of Defense Office of Local Defense Community Cooperation, *Defense Spending by State Fiscal Year 2020,* https://oldcc.gov/sites/default/files/defense-spending-rpts/OLDCC_DSBS_FY2020_FINAL_WEB.pdf.

36 Amanda Loder, "Keene Crib Company Adds Jobs Thanks To New Defense Contract (Really)," *StateImpact,* NPR, October 23, 2012, https://stateimpact.npr.org/new-hampshire/2012/10/23/keene-crib-company-adds-jobs-thanks-to-new-defense-contract-really/.

37 To enlarge this map and see captions, go to: https://www.google.com/maps/d/edit?mid=1DW10hd6cE7XmFuNIrycFLEShv7f0RtE-&usp=sharing.

38 John Ismay, "Carving Thousands of Headstones for the Fallen," *The New York Times Magazine,* September 23, 2018, https://www.nytimes.com/interactive/2018/09/23/magazine/those-who-cant-forget-headstones.html

39 From the Code of Federal Regulations [*National Archives,* https://www.ecfr.gov/current/title-13/chapter-I/part-124/subpart-A/subject-group-ECFR4ef1291a4a984ab/section-124.103]: "There is a rebuttable presumption that the following individuals are socially disadvantaged: Black Americans; Hispanic Americans; Native Americans (Alaska Natives, Native Hawaiians, or enrolled members of a Federally or State recognized Indian Tribe); Asian Pacific Americans (persons with origins from Burma, Thailand, Malaysia, Indonesia, Singapore, Brunei, Japan, China (including Hong Kong), Taiwan, Laos, Cambodia (Kampuchea), Vietnam, Korea, The Philippines, U.S. Trust Territory of the Pacific Islands (Republic of Palau), Republic of the Marshall Islands, Federated States of Micronesia, the Commonwealth of the Northern Mariana Islands, Guam, Samoa, Macao, Fiji, Tonga, Kiribati, Tuvalu, or Nauru); Subcontinent Asian Americans (persons with origins from India, Pakistan, Bangladesh, Sri Lanka, Bhutan, the Maldives Islands or Nepal); and members of other groups designated from time to time by SBA according to procedures set forth at paragraph (d) of this section. Being born in a country does not, by itself, suffice to make the birth country an individual's country of origin for purposes of being included within a designated group."

40 U.S. Department of Defense, Office of Small Business Programs, https://business. defense.gov/.

41 U.S. Small Business Administration, Office of the HUBZone Program, https:// www.sba.gov/about-sba/sba-locations/headquarters-offices/office-hubzone- program.

42 L3Harris, "L3Harris 2021 Diversity, Equity and Inclusion Annual Report," https:// www.l3harris.com/resources/l3harris-2021-diversity-equity-and-inclusion-annual- report.

43 Ibid.

44 Ibid.

45 Ibid.

46 CareerSource Florida, "Governor DeSantis Announces Launch of Lockheed Martin, CareerSource Florida Apprenticeship Program," *Cision PR Newswire,* February 24, 2021, https://www.prnewswire.com/news-releases/governor-desantis- announces-launch-of-lockheed-martin-careersource-florida-apprenticeship- program-301235029.html.

47 Alice Speri, "Blackwater Founder Erik Prince Sues The Intercept Over Russian Mercenary Report," *The Intercept,* December 2, 2021, https://theintercept. com/2021/12/02/erik-prince-blackwater-lawsuit-intercept/.

48 "Academi, Triple Canopy and 5 other Companies Merge forming the Largest High Threat Security Group in the World," *POC,* June 13, 2014, https://www.your-poc. com/academi-triple-canopy-5-companies-merge-forming-largest-high-threat- security-group-world/.

49 Ibid.

50 "Spending by Prime Award" (table), *USASpending.gov,* https://www.usaspending. gov/search/?hash=ef06e8c7ad3a7d3cccc2ca92b5c710d3.

51 Pierre Bélanger and Alexander Arroyo, *Ecologies of Power: Countermapping the Logistical Landscapes & Military Geographies of the U.S. Department of Defense* (Cambridge, MA: MIT Press, 2016), 93.

52 Reed Parker, "Ameriqual Packaging Secures Military Contract," *Inside Indiana Business,* November 3, 2021, https://www.insideindianabusiness.com/articles/ ameriqual-packaging-secures-military-contract.

53 Ameriqual Foods, "AmeriQual Proudly Supports Our Warfighters," https://www. ameriqual.com/military/.

54 MRE 39 (2019) menus, https://www.dla.mil/Portals/104/Documents/TroopSupport/ Subsistence/Rations/MRE/MREmenus.pdf?ver=2017-10-13-100714-227.

55 Defense Logistics Agency, "Humanitarian Daily Ration (HDR)," https://www.dla. mil/TroopSupport/Subsistence/Operational-rations/hdr/.

56 Propper, "About Us," https://www.propper.com/about-us.

57 Winvale, "What is the Berry Amendment?," https://info.winvale.com/blog/what-is- the-berry-amendment.

58 Burlington Fabrics, "Burlington operates in three global locations - USA, Mexico, and China," https://www.burlingtonfabrics.com/global-locations/.

59 "Advanced Undersea Warfare Systems" by Systems Engineering Analysis Cohort 17, Team B, June 2011, https://nps.edu/documents/105988579/106076806/SEA- 17B_Final_Report.pdf/a558e73f-c02a-411d-82d8-53aa84286421.

60 Battelle Facebook page, https://www.facebook.com/Battelle/.

61 The Voices and Faces Project, https://voicesandfaces.org/.

62 Fair Labor Association profile, *GuideStar,* https://www.guidestar.org/profile/52-2183112.
63 Focus HOPE, https://focushope.edu/about-focus-hope/.
64 Partners Achieving Success CDC Inc. profile, *GuideStar,* https://www.guidestar.org/profile/20-2393044.

CHAPTER FOUR

UNIVERSITIES AND RESEARCH INSTITUTES

POLITICAL CULTURE: PACIFISM AND MILITARISM

American political culture is heavily shaped by its major intellectual and technological institutions. With few exceptions, there is silence about our present or recent wars, whether traditional or "unconventional," and the human and environmental costs of our preparation for endless warfare. It wasn't always the case that antiwar voices could be silenced. During the 19th century, Enlightenment thought and radical Christianity both fostered a respectable antiwar current in the intellectual environment. Most of the communitarian societies in the northern and western United States, whether religious or socialist, were strongly pacifist—although their sites were often on lands that had previously been violently seized from indigenous peoples. Until 1914, antiwar theologians, artists and writers, and even politicians and businesspeople, were held in high esteem by the general population. Social science was slowly developing with the goal of producing happiness for humanity.

However, there was always another current, unfortunately the dominant one. Science, technology, and medicine had throughout history been in service to the military, which supported the individuals and institutions producing such knowledge. Liberal arts scholars and universities, even those of religious persuasion, celebrated the extermination of indigenous peoples, the war of independence, the Civil War, and the colonial expansion resulting from the Spanish-American War.

Large-scale federal government support of higher education swelled the military current:

> The American military's relationship with universities and colleges began in almost an absence of mind. It arose from an afterthought stipulation in the Morrill

95

Land-Grant College Act of 1862 that institutions to be financed under the terms of the act through income from the sale of federal lands must offer military training as part of the curriculum. For three-quarters of a century, little of note developed from this beginning, but following World War II, the university-military collaboration became a vital feature of American society. Amid the unending tensions of the postwar era, Americans' call for their universities to service national policy priorities—especially some that required or made use of secrecy and deception—would put at risk higher education's own priorities for promoting honest and independent scholarship and teaching.[1]

Still, there were those who were revolted by the horrors of the U.S. Civil War and the European wars of the 19th century. Prominent intellectuals and politicians gathered at The Hague, Netherlands in 1899 and 1907 to produce historical declarations against war.

Yet, in the early 20th century, those opposing U.S. participation in World War I faced severe repression, and pacifism was no longer respectable. Nevertheless, many worldwide continued to believe that war was obsolete, and an abomination. The Kellogg-Briand Pact of 1928 sought to eliminate war as an instrument of national policy. It was signed by most of the world's nations, but didn't provide for effective enforcement, and was soon to be drowned out by fascist militarism. The fascist glorification of violence and the military threat it posed persuaded many that war was essential, inevitable, and must be pursued despite the horrible consequences.

Henceforth, those who opposed war, such as Secretary of State Frank Kellogg, were called "isolationists." While the religion-based universities and colleges in the U.S. were rarely infused with pacifism, they gradually became secularized and part of the mainstream. New universities founded by industrialists, e.g., the University of Chicago, Johns Hopkins, and Stanford, were usually from the outset advocates of national expansionism. Another damper on pacifism were the socialists and anti-colonial activists worldwide who were admirers of the French and Russian Revolutions, and regarded the violent path as the only route to freedom and progress.

UNIVERSITY-MILITARY PARTNERSHIPS

During WWII, the Manhattan Project to develop an atom bomb was a collaboration of government, industry, and universities. Laboratories at Berkeley, Columbia University, University of Chicago, and Massachusetts Institute of Technology supplied crucial experimental research. Scientists came to Los Alamos from Cornell, Stanford, Purdue, University of Rochester, University of Illinois, Washington University, and Princeton.[2] This type of collaboration became a model for partnerships during the Cold War. The large foundations now also played a part, for this effort emphasized "unconventional" warfare, with ideology and subversion major strategies.

Manhattan Project   Source: Wikimedia Commons

With the 1947 creation of the National Security Council and the Central Intelligence Agency many academic disciplines became active participants in the Cold War. New institutes were sponsored, such as the Russian Research Center at Harvard, the European Institute at Columbia, and the Center for International Studies at Massachusetts Institute of Technology.

These new international policy disciplines and "area studies" (e.g., Asian Studies) were provided with an avalanche of facilities—buildings, libraries, computer technology. Staffs and faculties were assembled, granted unprecedented autonomy and exalted in one jump to a kind of penthouse status in the academic hierarchy. They were provided freedom and leverage by abundant outside financing. With all of this backing, they quickly became the most powerful influence on the old horse-and-buggy departments whose disciplines and concepts of scholarship began to follow the winning model set before them.[3]

The work was attractive for other than economic reasons. The programs had a club-like atmosphere, scholars were permitted to publish unclassified parts of their research, and could rationalize that their work subverting or converting communist or "developing" nations would obviate the need to nuke them.

National security-university covert collaborations ranged far and wide. Among the most notable: the International Cooperation Administration (forerunner of U.S. Agency for International Development) contract with Michigan State University to train the "police" in Vietnam, and the CIA sponsorship of lysergic acid diethylamide (LSD) experiments on volunteer subjects in the Psychology Department of New York University. Also: "In the mid-1950s, professors at MIT and Cornell launched field projects in Indonesia to train elite Indonesian military and economic leaders who would ultimately launch the coup that brought Suharto to power and left over one million people dead."[4] Generally, only the principal investigator knew of the real source of the projects; other professors and students were unwitting.

ACADEMIC DISSENTERS

Collaborations proceeded without noticeable dissent until the Vietnam War, the exposure of U.S. Army Project Camelot of 1964, and the revelation of covert CIA funding of university programs and scholarly associations in 1967. Camelot was a counterinsurgency program that employed social scientists to collect cultural and social process information in foreign countries. Anthropologist Catherine Lutz wrote:

> Counterinsurgency planners tell us that human thinking and affect are the primary terrain which must be mapped and conquered in order to defeat or convert the enemy, or to at least render the surrounding population

neutral in that struggle of wills which is called counterinsurgency war.[5]

Although government agencies' social scientists were involved, many studies were contracted out, and the academic participants were often unaware of the sponsor. The research was usually classified, which contravened the norms of academic freedom. Protests by academics, especially anthropologists, curtailed the program, but similar ones were then undertaken with mitigating procedures, such as allowing more research to be unclassified.

Subsequent programs, especially the Human Terrain System (HTS) of 2007, which engaged social scientists in obtaining sociocultural, anthropologic and ethnographic data in Iraq and Afghanistan, were protested loudly. Anthropologist Roberto J. González noted that HTS personnel also aided interrogations, and that the program was used to influence U.S. citizens:

> It became a propaganda tool for convincing the American public—especially those with liberal tendencies—that the U.S.-led occupations of Iraq and Afghanistan were benevolent missions in which smart, fresh-faced young college graduates were playing a role. It appeared to demonstrate how U.S. forces were engaged in a kinder, gentler form of occupation. Department of Defense photos portrayed HTS personnel sitting on rugs while drinking tea with Afghan elders, or distributing sweets to euphoric Iraqi children. Here was a war that Americans could feel good about fighting.[6]

Presaging the current multinational military-industrial complex, major contractors for the HTS were BAE Systems (a British-owned weapons corporation) and CGI Federal (Canadian Information Technology consultants).

Among other protests, the American Anthropological Association issued a statement condemning the program and it was officially closed in 2014. However, although the "unconventional wars" employing scholars of diverse disciplines continued, protest was muted after 9/11. The American Anthropological Association had adopted an ethics code, requiring that populations studied must give voluntary informed consent, research must not be intended to convert those studied, et al, and it was on these grounds alone that most opposition persisted, not "because it assists the American military in an unjust project of empire, occupation, and exploitation."[7]

Nevertheless, a small number of anthropologists have continued their opposition to weaponizing their discipline, including Catherine Lutz, now co-director of The Costs of War project at The Watson Institute, Brown University, and David Price, author of *Weaponizing Anthropology.*

In 1967, political scientists at the annual American Political Science Association convention noted the absence of any panels on the Vietnam War. This prompted the formation of the Caucus for New Political Science, in hopes of making such relevant issues a recognized part of political science scholarship. Another aim was to investigate how foundations were setting the agenda for political scientists. Gradually, the Caucus developed a broader focus on social justice and identity politics, and never developed as a primarily antiwar protest. There was little comprehensive research on the connections between the APSA, universities, foundations, and the national security state. Now the Caucus describes its mission as "the idea that political science as an academic discipline should be committed to advancing progressive political development."[8]

Other disciplines in the social sciences and humanities formed radical caucuses in the 1960s; they still exist but are now very quiet. The 1969 protest at the Massachusetts Institute of Technology was a rare occurrence in the heart of the military university contractor world.

> The Union of Concerned Scientists [UCS] was founded in 1969 by scientists and students at the Massachusetts Institute of Technology. That year, the Vietnam War was at its height and Cleveland's heavily polluted Cuyahoga River had caught fire. Appalled at how the United States government was misusing science, the UCS founders ... drafted a statement calling for scientific research to be directed away from military technologies and toward solving pressing environmental and social problems.[9]

Again in the 1980s, there was concern at MIT about military research; some scientists objected to working on the Strategic Defense Initiative (SDI), known as "Star Wars." In a 1989 volume of *The Annals of the American Academy of Political and Social Science* devoted to "Universities and the Military" a MIT Physics professor, Vera Kistiakowsky, was a rare dissenter. She wrote: "DoD funding of university research has consequences for the university, the students, and the nation, and it has no benefits that could not be achieved with other funding sources."[10] She also reiterated the UCS argument:

> The preferential funding of weapons programs has had its
> economic consequences, witnessed by our deteriorating
> civilian industrial infrastructure, our negative balance
> of trade, and our mounting deficit. We have not invested
> in civilian research at a level adequate to these pressing
> problems, and will continue to suffer the consequences
> until we do.[11]

In 2022, when most scientists had long been silent, the Episcopal Chaplain division of MIT held a major conference: "Reducing the Threat of Nuclear War: Rebuilding a Broader Movement." It was co-sponsored by major peace groups of the U.S. and their leaders were featured speakers.

Throughout the Vietnam War there were faculty and student protests at many colleges and universities, albeit with weak participation beyond the social sciences and humanities. A major feature was the "teach-in" movement to raise awareness of what was happening. On the next page is the announcement of one such, taken from my own experience.

There were also demonstrations, marches, and direct action, which did break the silence. The extent to which activists influenced the change of policy is still being debated, but surely it is a necessary first step for politicians and the public to become aware of the nation's policies and their consequences. The loudest protest was at Kent State University, Ohio. And there, in 1970, 4 students were killed and 9 wounded by members of the Ohio National Guard during an anti–Vietnam war rally.

TEACH-IN ON THE ISSUES IN VIETNAM[12]

Wednesday night, April 14, 1965, New York University—University College Playhouse, Gould Student Center, West 18lst Street and University Avenue, the Bronx, doors open 7:45 p.m.

8:00   Philip G. Zimbardo (NYU) , chairman,
        Prof. Seymour Melman, Columbia University,
        "A Strategy for Peace."

8:50   Dr. Vo Thanh Minh, "The South Vietnamese Position"

9:15   Prof. Amitai Etzioni, Columbia University,
        "Which Way Out?"

10:15   Constance R. Sutton (NYU), chairman,
        Prof. Robert Engler, Queens College,
        "The United States and the World in Revolution"

11:00   Prof. Ernest van den Haag, New York University, "Is
        Intervention for Freedom Justified?"

12:00   Joan Fiss [Roelofs] (NYU), chairman,
        Raymond Brown, Sarah Lawrence College, "The
        Domestic Economic Implications of the Cold War"

12:45   Prof. Anthony J. Pearce, New York University,
        "How Did the United States Become Involved in
        Vietnam: 1954–60?"

1:45   Roscoe C. Brown, Jr. (NYU) , chairman,
        Mr. Ross Flannagan, New York Friends Group, "The Moral
        and Human Dimensions of the War in Vietnam"

2:30   Michael Arons (NYU) , chairman,
        Prof. James T. Crown, New York University
        "The Great War or the Great Society?"

3:15   Prof. Stanley Millet, Briarcliff College,
        "American Policy in Vietnam"

Sponsors: Ad Hoc Faculty Committee on Vietnam, New York University.

Cochairmen: Philip G. Zimbardo, Constance R . Sutton; Robert D. Burrowes; Edwin S. Campbell; James T. Crown; Joan Fiss [Roelofs]; H. Mark Roelofs; H. Laurence Ross; and Thomas W. Wahman.

ANTIWAR PROTEST FADES

Gradually, silence descended. Protest against war, empire, and capitalism was channeled, with major assistance from foundation funding,
into identity politics and featured single issue nongovernmental organizations (NGOS).[13] Universities had become used to the juicy contracts,
enabling the construction of new facilities and new hires. Students were
attracted to the well-funded departments and programs, which became
even more attractive when heavy student loan debt became the norm.

Scholarships and internships are very attractive to today's ca-
reer-minded students. Those offered by military contractors in partnership with organizations such as the American Association of University
Women led some to argue that engaging women in military work is a
feminist triumph.

While scholarship programs for minorities, such as the NAACP
ACT-SO (Afro-Academic, Cultural, Technological and Scientific
Olympics), are effective contributions to integrating our national elites,
they also enhance public relations for the weapons corporations that donate. Scholars receiving federal government fellowships (e.g., from the
National Endowment for the Humanities, National Science Foundation,
and Fulbright programs) are required to report to the national security
apparatus, according to the well-funded National Security Education
Act of 1992. Although a few academic associations refused to cooper-
ate, most do.

The physical sciences, engineering, mathematics, business, and
communications faculties and students had never been prominent among
the protestors, and now these departments have been enlarged, thanks
to DoD and contractor funding, at the expense of social science and
humanities. In addition, biology, psychology, and environmental studies
now have military contracts; everything requires threat mobilization,
according to the DoD.

What remains of the social sciences and humanities must also be
swayed. Contractor donations to higher education now include many
disciplines and professional schools:

> [Master of Social Work] student Sara Bovat receives
> a surprising message: The School of Social Service
> Administration at the University of Chicago is changing
> its name to the Crown Family School of Social Work,

Policy, and Practice, in recognition of a $75 million donation from James and Paula Crown. When she finds out James Crown is director of the board for General Dynamics Corp., the third-largest defense contractor in the United States, her surprise turns to outrage. "To think that our social work school would be named after a family that profits off of the military-industrial complex just felt very hypocritical," Bovat says.[14]

Despite such occasional protests, after 9/11, the militarization of higher education was mostly accepted, if not cheered.

ROTC, University of Florida, 1920s   Source: Creative Commons, UF Digital

RESERVE OFFICER TRAINING CORPS (ROTC)

Reserve Officer Training Corps (ROTC) programs, required at land-grant institutions, have long existed in most colleges and universities, today numbering 1,700 institutions. For example, in Massachusetts there are programs at Boston University, Massachusetts Institute of Technology, Northeastern University, University of Massachusetts, and Worcester Polytechnic Institute. However, students at Harvard, Berklee School of Music, Emerson, Hampshire, Smith and all the other colleges in Massachusetts can enroll in ROTC and take the training at the major institutions.[15] In exchange for paid tuition graduates are committed to serve in the military. The military courses are taught by officers, while the students join with the others for their civilian education. Many do not complete the ROTC programs or go on to become officers, but they have had exposure to the military point of view, and often considerable amounts of free tuition.

MILITARIZED UNIVERSITIES

VICE News compiled a list of the "100 most militarized universities in America," measured by:

> university labs funded by U.S. intelligence agencies, administrators with strong ties to those same agencies, and, most importantly, the educational backgrounds of the approximately 1.4 million people who hold Top Secret clearance in the United States ... The 100 schools named in the VICE News rankings produce the greatest number of students who are employed by the Intelligence Community (IC), have the closest relationships with the national security state, and profit the most from American war waging.... [Their sample] includes military and law enforcement personnel, government civilian employees, and contractors at the federal, state, and local levels.[16]

While twenty of these institutions are mostly unknown—VICE considers them "online diploma mills"—some famous ones are also included, ranked in this order:

1. University of Maryland
2. American Military University
3. University of Phoenix
4. George Washington University
5. George Mason University
6. Cochise College
7. Johns Hopkins University
8. Strayer University
9. Webster University
10. Georgetown University[17]

Northern Virginia Community College is at number 16, Harvard at 32, and surprisingly, Norwich University is at 46 and MIT at 47. MIT in most years has been the educational institution with the largest funding in DoD contracts, but the varied destinations of its graduates may have lowered its rank. Norwich, one of the Senior Military Colleges, has long been a private military university and years ago was involved in a major scandal because of its training of Indonesian special forces.

INTELLIGENCE COMMUNITY PROGRAMS AND SCHOLARSHIPS

A more recent program spreading military wealth and culture even further into higher education, particularly aimed at institutions attended by low income and minority students, is the Intelligence Community Centers for Academic Excellence (IC CAE) Program.

> [It] was established in 2005 to meet the nation's demand for a diverse cadre of professionals to carry out national security priorities and obligations. The IC requires a diverse, professionally competitive and knowledgeable workforce to successfully accomplish its mission. The intent of the IC CAE Program is to increase the pool of competitive, diverse applicants, and to increase awareness of the IC mission and culture throughout ethnically and geographically diverse communities. While all accredited four-year colleges and universities in the United States are eligible, the legislation emphasizes increased IC workforce gender, ethnic, and geographic (rural) diversity. It also compels the program to award grants to applicants that are either "part of a consortium or specifically enhance collaboration with under-resourced schools in a manner that promotes diversity."[18]

The program exists at many state, city, and private universities and colleges, community colleges, and includes the City College of New York, once a hotbed of socialist disputation.

> IC CAE scholars study intelligence-related curricula, learn from faculty who are offered specialized training and

research opportunities, and participate in workshops, simulations, conferences and seminars. During the seminar, IC CAE scholars from across the country meet with legislators, IC agencies and National Intelligence Managers. They also participate in a simulation that replicates a real-world intelligence problem to enhance students' critical thinking, analytic and tradecraft skills. College and Universities with IC CAE programs receive funding to support: Curriculum development; Faculty professional development and research; Student study abroad, and participation in Intelligence-related conferences and seminars; Delivery of on-site intelligence-related workshops, simulations and practical exercises.[19]

A DoD program in Cybersecurity with similar vast participation is managed by the National Security Agency.

An *advocate* of the university-military partnership, Matthew D. Crosston has said:

> Whether considering the impact of the PATRIOT ACT on civil liberties, moral debates about "black prisons" and Guantanamo Bay, the inability to formally remove all American troops from inside Iraq and Afghanistan, the Edward Snowden affair, or informally using weaponized drones in over a half-dozen countries experiencing internal turmoil, ample evidence is available for today's faculty to focus on if they are looking for reasons to resist collaboration and cooperation.[20]

Nevertheless, Crosston gives several reasons to support such collaboration:

> Finally, if students should be discouraged from pursuing employment with organizations that have questionable histories in ethical and moral decision making, then universities should refrain from promoting programs that connect to Economics and Business. Should banking, real estate, and Internet entrepreneurship be eliminated from

study? Over the last two decades, few industries have displayed such "sordid" moral and ethical pasts.[21]

Accordingly, he sees the good of university-military cooperation as far outweighing the bad, putting it this way:

> Yet the reality is that such collaboration has helped deepen the accuracy of intelligence analysis, thus arguably leading to the development of positive policy changes that alleviate suffering around the globe rather than contribute to it.[22]

ACADEMIC RESEARCH

The militarization of academic research has spread far and wide. Most publicized instances are the contracts and grants for weapons and information technology. The Massachusetts Institute of Technology (MIT) usually leads the pack with annual funding about a billion. So as not to be redundant, this aspect of the MIC will not be detailed here; it has been well covered in Christian Sorenson's *Understanding the War Industry,* Nicolas Turse's *The Complex* (2008), and Henry Giroux's "The Politics of Higher Education and the Militarized Academy after 9/11."[23]

In the hard and soft sciences, research is often conducted by the DoD's many in-house scientists and engineers, and also consortia that may include other federal departments and agencies, industry, academia, nonprofits, and international scholars. For example, the Information Warfare Research Project has members from large information technology companies such as Accenture and Amazon, from Southern Methodist University and University of Florida, and from nonprofits such as the Draper Laboratory. The Charles Stark Draper Laboratory was originally part of MIT, but became an independent institution because of protest by some MIT faculty opposing war research.

To insure that no state is left behind, the DoD has initiated the Defense Established Program to Stimulate Competitive Research, to find "underrepresented U.S. states and territories for researchers with important contributions to [DOD's] scientific enterprise."[24]

DEFENSE ADVANCED RESEARCH PROJECTS AGENCY

In its depth, military research goes far beyond conventional, nuclear, and cyber weapons. The Defense Advanced Research Projects Agency (DARPA) biodefense strategy program, PREventing EMerging Pathogenic Threats (PREEMPT), contracts with teams modeling specific diseases to assess the risk of spillover from animals into human contacts. The teams include, among many others, the Australian Animal Health Laboratory, the University of California, the University of Glasgow, Institut Pasteur, University of Cambridge, University of Tartu (Estonia), the Pirbright Institute (UK), and Cornell University.[25] As many scientists have pointed out, biosafety research can also be used for biowarfare weaponry.

DARPA takes pride in advancing "military capabilities such as precision weapons and stealth technology" but it also claims major contributions to "modern civilian society such as the Internet, automated voice recognition and language translation, and Global Positioning System receivers small enough to embed in myriad consumer devices."[26]

While endless illegal wars of choice have created many amputees and mentally disturbed soldiers, DARPA emphasizes its humanitarianism in devising scientific solutions for both injured veterans and civilians. In 2019 it stated:

> Over the past 18 years, DARPA has demonstrated increasingly sophisticated neurotechnologies that rely on surgically implanted electrodes to interface with the central or peripheral nervous systems. The agency has demonstrated achievements such as neural control of prosthetic limbs and restoration of the sense of touch to the users of those limbs, relief of otherwise intractable neuropsychiatric illnesses such as depression, and improvement of memory formation and recall.[27]

More recently it has contracted with researchers at the University of North Carolina and Stanford to study "Certain drugs such as LSD and psilocybin [that] exhibit hallucinogenic effects, but have also have potential for the treatment of depression, anxiety, and substance abuse."[28] This brings to mind an earlier series of experiments for weaponizing LSD, secretly funded in the 1950s by the CIA, and carried out by the Psychology Department at New York University, among other sites.

Another project with military intentions and civilian extensions employs scientists at the University of California-Davis, Johns Hopkins University, and the University of Pittsburgh.

> Multidisciplinary teams at each of these universities are tasked with developing systems of implantable, adaptive devices that aim to reduce injury effects during early phases of [Spinal Cord Injuries] SCI, and potentially restore function during the later chronic phase.[29]

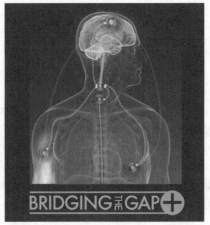

Implantable Device   Source: DoD / DARPA

However, DARPA has sponsored extensive research in neurotechnology intended to create cyborgs for military uses. While DARPA's work with insect cyborgs has been buzzing along for years, its plans for human enhancement are even more spectacular. One aim is to enable humans to control weapons with their thoughts. Currently, humans remotely control drones via computers; the cyborg is intended to eliminate that external step. Electrodes would be placed on the skull or invasively implanted on the brain.

> This technology is predicted to facilitate read/write capability between humans and machines and between humans through brain-to-brain interactions. These interactions would allow warfighters direct communication with unmanned and autonomous systems, as well as with

other humans, to optimize command and control systems and operations. The potential for direct data exchange between human neural networks and microelectronic systems could revolutionize tactical warfighter communications, speed the transfer of knowledge throughout the chain of command, and ultimately dispel the "fog" of war. Direct neural enhancement of the human brain through neuro-silica interfaces could improve target acquisition and engagement and accelerate defensive and offensive systems.[30]

DARPA is now using social media, via its Polyplexus site to attract more researchers to its projects:

The platform facilitates connections among experts across academic disciplines so they can propel novel research opportunities together. Beta-launched for academics only in 2018, Polyplexus is now open to the broader research and development community and features an initial offering of research topics for collaboration and potential funding. DARPA seeks participation from anyone who is interested in sharing and learning about emerging science and technology including researchers, practitioners, and even retirees.[31]

DARPA's futuristic research (e.g., insect drones, cyborgs) is attractive to scientific minds. Children have been inundated with praise for science's military application, as elementary and high schools, as well as youth organizations, offer Science, Technology, Engineering and Math (STEM) education funded by military contractors and the DoD.

Any discipline may be relevant to national security. A DARPA contract employed a social psychology professor with a specialization in religion, Kathryn Johnson, for a study: "Developing and Signaling Trust in Synthetic Autonomous Agents."[32] DARPA research has indicated that religious people worldwide are often opposed to using robots and cyborgs for warfare, and this opposition is a threat to military plans, so ways of countering this threat must be discovered by social scientists.

MINERVA RESEARCH INITIATIVE

While scholars in many disciplines pursue classified research for DARPA, other DoD agencies, and the Intelligence Advanced Research Projects Activity (IARPA), the Minerva Research Initiative was created to allay the criticism of military secrecy, so its projects are unclassified. Most of the principal investigators are based at U.S. universities, but some are at foreign ones, and teamwork, often international, is encouraged.[33] Political science researchers are heavily represented.

Recent Minerva projects include "Russia's malign influence campaigns," which baldly suggests that we must avoid our "demonstrably ineffective practices as countering disinformation with truth and evidence." Another claims that military deployments overseas "other than invasions" lead foreigners to have a more positive view of the U.S. Still another seeks to determine how the U.S. can deal with the threat to its global leadership from "rising power alliances."

Geographers have been part of a project mapping indigenous lands in Honduras, and were given the justification that participatory mapping can help indigenous people maintain control over their lands. However, geographer Joel Wainwright has argued:

> We show, first, that the Minerva program that funded the Bowman Expedition to Honduras is a program of the U.S. military, intended to increase the power of the U.S. military through the development of novel tactics, data, and weapons via collaboration with civilian social scientists; second, that awards from the Minerva program are not based principally upon standard scholarly evaluation, but upon expected returns to the U.S. military; and third, that the authors … knew these first two points prior to speaking to their indigenous interlocutors, because their funding proposal to the Minerva program promised benefits to the U.S. military.[34]

Despite the enthusiastic publicity and the generous funding, the U.S. Joint Forces Command isn't very impressed with the results. One of its early Minerva program evaluators said "Most seem to be empty exercises in pedanticism, devoid of context or relevance."[35]

Another assessment of Minerva by the National Academy of Sciences stated:

> [E]valuating a program's causal effects requires an analysis of the "counterfactual," that is, estimation of what would have happened in the absence of the program. The committee determined that the available data were not adequate for this.[36]

Nevertheless, it was positive about the program and the dissemination of its research in scholarly publications and to non-academic audiences via *"The New York Times, The Washington Post, Foreign Affairs Snapshots, Scientific American, The Atlantic, Cipher Brief, The Wire, McLeans, The National Interest,* and *Politico,* as well as international publications."*[37]

DoD staff members among the evaluators wondered if social scientists might stay away from national security funded research because it could harm their professional reputation. However, the consensus did not find this a problem.

> When grantees were asked about challenges associated with conducting (unclassified) research relevant to national security, only 12 percent mentioned criticism from academic colleagues due to DoD funding, which suggests that these types of concerns are not pervasive.[38]

On the other hand, a Social Science Research Council symposium conducted at the outset of the Minerva Initiative found apprehension among some scholars. Professor Catherine Lutz stated it plainly:

> The first [danger] is that the Pentagon frames the questions to be asked and decides which independently framed questions are sensible or important, and does both these things within the constraints of what C. Wright Mills years ago called the military definition of reality. This entails seeing the world as a series of threats to be dealt with, sorting people into enemies and allies, and focusing on the use or threat of force—physical (missile and machine gun fire), mental (psychological operations,

public relations campaigns), and financial (enforcement of sanctions, bribery of local actors, arms deals).[39]

Another symposium participant, Prof. Ronald Krebs, later warned: "Academic freedom, ... seeks to free scholars from self-censorship as well, which can result not only from the fear of sticks but also from the lure of carrots."[40] Thus echoing the concern of Prof. Lutz:

> Faculty with Pentagon funding would have a leg up in re-
> cruiting graduate students, curricula would replace some
> existing courses..., and university administrators would
> reward, as they now do, those who bring in the money,
> public attention, and political connections that funding
> on high status subjects provides. Other, more pressing
> research and researchers will undergo a brain drain. The
> spaces for critique of war as a social practice will continue
> to contract.[41]

The utility of the research findings may be minor, but the program can still be very useful to the military. There is more trickle down than trickle up. Academics come under the wing of the military budget, and they are not likely to flutter their connection too noticeably or look too closely—certainly not critically—at the worldwide operations of our armed forces. An international elite of DoD and NATO funded scholars will see their sponsors' aims as necessary and proper, and are likely to convey a militarized view of human and state interactions to the media, politicians, and the younger generation of students.

THE WORLDWIDE FUNDING OF DOD RESEARCH

The worldwide funding of DoD research is not much publicized. It could be a factor in the considerable silence, even in social demo-cratic nations, related to opposition to U.S. wars and their prepara-tion. Outsourcing is not done to save money, but to supplement local knowledge with the brains of the world, and indeed, to penetrate their countries' institutions. Thus, a worldwide network of DoD collaborators is created, comprised of scientific elites in many countries having a cozy relationship with the U.S. military who may have considerable influence on their nation's politics and educational systems.

Nuclear, Chemical, and Biological Defense
Cooperative Biological Engagement Program Country Engagements

GHSA Phase 1
Cameroon
Cote D'Ivoire
Ethiopia
Guinea
India
Indonesia
Kenya
Liberia
Mali
Pakistan
Sierra Leone
Senegal
Tanzania
Uganda
Vietnam

GHSA Phase 2
Cambodia
Georgia
Jordan
Laos
Malaysia
Thailand
Ukraine
Kazakhstan

Additional
Afghanistan
Armenia
Azerbaijan
Iraq
Philippines
South Africa
Uzbekistan

Worldwide Biological Research

Source: DoD[42]

Contracts and consortia are heavy in the fields of information technology, nanotechnology, biotechnology, and weapons, but anything goes. Universities, institutes, laboratories, and scientists are employed in Kenya, France, UK, Peru, New Zealand, Thailand, Republic of Georgia, and elsewhere in furtherance of the U.S. national security mission. Some examples: "Engineering of highly proficient catalytic bioscavengers for in vivo detoxification of a broad spectrum of nerve agents" (Israel); "Behavioural ecology of cetaceans" (Scotland); "Training . . . animal health professionals in epidemiology which will enhance the ability to prepare for and respond to disease outbreaks" (Laos).[43]

Here's an illustration of the diversity and likely influence of DoD foreign funding as operational at the King's College London Institute of Psychiatry.

> At the request of U.S. prosecution lawyers, Dr. Blackwood examined Assange during two meetings in March [2020]. In his written submission to the court, he said that it would 'not be unjust' to extradite Assange to the U.S.[44]

As pointed out by Matt Kennard and Mark Curtis in "Key Assange Prosecution Witness Part of Academic Cluster That Has Received Millions from UK & U.S. Militaries," Blackwood works in a unit at KCL that was originally funded by the U.S. DoD and remains associated with it.

ENVIRONMENTAL RESEARCH

Environmental protection and restoration is now a subject of interest to the military, and university researchers are in the consortia, focused more on studies about the "threat" to live-fire exercises and other missions coming *from* imperiled species and incompatible development, invasive species, and cetaceans (See Chapters 2 and 6).

Among the several environmental agencies in the DoD, the Strategic Environmental Research and Development Program has a broad range; it even sponsors studies of "Energy and Water Efficiency Improvements for Dishrooms in Military Dining Rooms."[45] Now we know that dishwashing has a role in greenwashing.

A surprising example of "spillover" is the Urban Dynamics Institute at Oakridge National Laboratory that was originally part of the

Manhattan Project. The Institute, while continuing as part of a high-tech military think tank, now claims it is an advanced laboratory for understanding, predicting, and resolving key urban problems. While this claim cannot be evaluated here, if there is truth in it, it is deplorable that essential research is not being provided by agencies unalloyed with the purveyors of lethality. The Oakridge Laboratory is currently engaged in the project of upgrading our nuclear weapons.

RESEARCH VIA NATO

The North Atlantic Treaty Organization (NATO), a strong arm of the U.S. military, has its own research programs, implemented in Western Europe and former iron curtain countries, now all under the uranium curtain. NATO has a huge bureaucracy of agencies and programs; researchers, instructors, and trainees are from both civilian and military sectors.

> The Science for Peace and Security (SPS) Programme promotes dialogue and practical cooperation between NATO member states and partner nations based on scientific research, technological innovation and knowledge exchange. [It funds research on the expected military topics, but also on] security issues arising from key environmental and resource constraints, including health risks, climate change, water scarcity and increasing energy needs, which have the potential to significantly affect NATO's planning and operations; disaster forecasting and prevention of natural catastrophes; and defence-related environmental issues.[46]

NATO has 33 Partnership Training and Education Centres, some in NATO member nations and others in partnership countries, which includes "Partnership for Peace" members such as Switzerland and Finland, and worldwide partners, for example Egypt, Mongolia, and Colombia. The inclusive reach of NATO's interests is evidenced in the Public Affairs Regional Centre in the Republic of North Macedonia, where it is to provide "Capacity Building in Public Affairs, instrumental for enhancing resilience and addressing vulnerabilities related to hybrid security threats such as disinformation and propaganda."[47]

Twenty-five NATO Centres of Excellence "train and educate leaders and specialists from NATO member and partner countries, assist in doctrine development, identify lessons learned, improve interoperability and capabilities, and test and validate concepts through experimentation."[48] For example, the NATO Strategic Communications Centre of Excellence based in Riga, Latvia:

> contributes to improved strategic communications capabilities within the Alliance and Allied nations. Strategic communication is an integral part of the efforts to achieve the Alliance's political and military objectives. The heart of the NATO StratCom COE is a diverse group of international experts with military, government and academic backgrounds—trainers, educators, analysts and researchers.[49]

A typical researcher, Dr. Una Aleksandra Bērziņa-Čerenkova, is the chair of the Political Science Doctoral Studies Programme at the Latvian Institute of International Affairs, reporting on "The People's Republic of China and The Russian Federation as Strategic Allies."[50]

NATIONAL SECURITY INSTITUTES

Scientists, engineers, and social scientists are employed directly by the DoD and CIA; others work in the national security institutes that are associated with universities, industry, and "think tanks," the supposedly independent nongovernmental organizations.

Job listings by the American Political Science Association indicate the variety of national security careers for political scientists.[51]

- U.S. Army War College
- University of Arizona Master of Arts Program in Global Security
- U.S. Air Force Academy
- Council on Foreign Relations
- U.S. Naval Academy
- The Clements Center for National Security at the University of Texas at Austin
- Virginia Military Institute

- University of Calgary (Canada) Post-Doctoral Scholar in National Defence and Data Analytics

National security institutes exist at many of our universities, such as George Mason, Stony Brook, Syracuse, and George Washington Universities, and even at community colleges. The old Cold War institutes are still around, often with a new name and an expanded focus; the Harvard Russian Research Center is now the Davis Center for Russian and Eurasian Studies.

> Retired military officers and national security officials often find hospitable homes in elite public policy institutions such as Yale's Jackson Institute, Harvard's Belfer Centre and Stanford's Hoover Institution. Junior and mid-career military officers benefit from these institutions too, thanks to generous endowments by captains of industry. Take, for example, the Recanati-Kaplan Foundation fellowship for intelligence officers at Harvard, or the Petraeus-Kaplan-Recanati fellowship for special operators at Yale....
>
> In the aftermath of each U.S. imperial war, without even a minimal reckoning like the Church Committee after the Vietnam War, the very people responsible for the wreckage of countries and the killing of millions swan on to the next lucrative assignment.[52]

A report by the Center for International Policy "U.S. Government and Defense Contractor Funding of America's Top 50 Think Tanks" noted that:

> Think tanks serve a specialized niche in the American political system. In theory, they're a bridge between academia and government. In practice, they can literally write our nation's laws and fill positions within the federal government. Think tanks are the political expert you see on TV and the author of that op-ed in your favorite paper. They are one of the key drivers of political discourse in America. Yet, despite this immense influence on

government and policy debates in the U.S., think tanks
are largely unknown to most Americans.[53]

Although think tanks are not required to report their donors, the
researchers unearthed this information and found that the top 10 recipients of government military and contractor funds from 2014–2019 were:

- RAND Corporation
- Center for a New American Security
- Atlantic Council
- New America Foundation
- German Marshall Fund of the United States
- Center for Strategic and International Studies
- Council on Foreign Relations
- Brookings Institution
- Heritage Foundation
- Stimson Center.[54]

The Council on Foreign Relations (CFR) and its influential journal, *Foreign Affairs,* are pre-eminent. Members include past, present
and future government officials and politicians (including most serious
presidential candidates), leading professors and journalists, foundation
and NGO people, and businesspeople. The CFR aims to project U.S.
power throughout the world, and to persuade U.S. citizens that this is in
the "national interest."

The Carnegie Endowment for International Peace (CEIP) is funded
by weapons corporations, IT military contractors such as Accenture,
the United States Indo-Pacific Command, North Atlantic Treaty
Organization Public Diplomacy Division, the Naval Postgraduate
School, the Defense Intelligence Agency, Cisco Systems, Open Society
Foundations, U.S. Department of Defense, General Electric, North
Atlantic Treaty Organization, and Lockheed Martin.[55] In the past it has
promoted "humanitarian intervention," "ousting foreign strongmen,"
and insuring that the United States "remains the leading military power."
Carnegie's journal, *Foreign Policy,* is intended to be accessible to con-
cerned citizens, progressive activists, and newspaper editors. A recent
article tells us that we need not fear the recent leftist victories in Latin
America; they will not threaten traditional U.S. policy:

Five Defense Contractors' Contributions to America's Top 50 Think Tanks

A Foreign Influence Transparency Initiative (FITI) investigation, *U.S. Government and Defense Contractor Funding of America's Top 50 Think Tanks*, tracked at least $1 billion in funding to the top 50 think tanks in America from 2014 to 2019.

Northrop Grumman, Boeing, Raytheon, Lockheed Martin, and Airbus contributed the most to top think tanks of all defense contractors, with line width indicating the size of the contribution.

Read the full report at internationalpolicy.org

CENTER FOR INTERNATIONAL POLICY
Advancing a peaceful, just, and sustainable world.

Think Tank Funding   Reprinted courtesy of CIP

> [M]any of the progressives riding this anti-incum-
> bent tsunami are pragmatic centrists who disfavor the
> timeworn, anti-imperialist rhetoric that burns bridges be-
> tween the United States and its neighbors.... [T]here are
> stark differences between progressive social democrats—
> including those with an old-school focus on social class
> and others who emphasize gender equality and renewable
> energy—and the unapologetic authoritarians in Cuba,
> Nicaragua, and Venezuela, who serve up Marxist rhetoric
> and ritualistic denunciations of U.S. imperialism.[56]

The Aspen Institute has long specialized in creating links between anti-poverty and minority organizations and the national security elite. James S. Crown, Chairman of the Aspen Institute Board of Trustees, is also the lead director of General Dynamics Corporation. Among its Lifetime Trustees are Madeleine K. Albright (now deceased) and Henry A. Kissinger. Major donors include military contractor Accenture, members of the Crown (General Dynamics) family, and the U.S. Agency for International Development.[57]

The Center for American Progress has close ties with Democratic presidential administrations. Its donors include General Electric, Boeing and Lockheed. Furthermore,

> Scott Lilly, ... who joined CAP in 2004 as a senior
> fellow covering national security simultaneously served
> as a registered lobbyist for Lockheed between 2005 and
> 2011. Rudy deLeon, CAP's senior vice president for na-
> tional security and international policy, was a Boeing ex-
> ecutive and directed the company's lobbying operations
> between 2001 and 2006, before joining the think tank the
> following year.[58]

U.S. INSTITUTE OF PEACE

The U.S. Institute of Peace (USIP) is a prime example of both silencing and militarization. It describes itself as a national, nonpartisan, independent institute, founded by Congress and dedicated to the proposition that a world without violent conflict is possible, practical and essential for U.S. and global security.[59] Among its partners are the U.S.

Departments of State and Defense, the USAID, NATO, and the Geneva Centre for Security Policy, along with the more appropriate American Friends Service Committee.[60]

A proposal for a Department of Peace to counterbalance the Department of War was promoted in the early 20th century when pacifism was still respectable. It did not get very far in Congress. In the 1970s, peace advocates proposed an Academy of Peace, to balance the U.S. military academies.

> Interestingly, several conservative lobbies joined the National Peace Academy Campaign (N-PAC) and made sure that radical groups would not be in the agenda-setting seat. The World Without War Council (WWWC), a CIA-affiliated 'peace' group, collected 90,000 signatures in favour of the Academy.... Cold war hawks favouring the Academy expected it to highlight human rights abuses under totalitarian states in the Soviet sphere and reconnect peace to democracy promotion....[61]

The Academy was intended to support peace studies in schools and universities, and thereby provide a counterweight to the burgeoning "national security" degrees and institutes. This didn't fly with President Reagan and Congress. However, in 1984 Congress created the Institute of Peace as a concession to the antiwar movement, which at the time had both grassroots support and outspoken advocates who held highly respectable positions in our nation. The President and Congress immediately attempted to water down the Institute's potential. "When these sabotage efforts failed, Reagan infiltrated the Institute with a Board of white males with ultra-conservative backgrounds..."[62]

So it remains today, except that one need not be a white male. U.S. foreign policy at home and throughout the world earns greater respect when the face behind it is female or minority. The current (2022) USIP 15-member board of directors includes 3 members ex officio— representatives of these entities are always on the board—Lloyd Austin, Secretary of Defense (or his designee), Tony Blinken, Secretary of State, State Department (or his designee) and Major General Gregory S. Martin, President, National Defense University. About half of the other 12 members of the Institute Board are part of the national security establishment, several having served on the National Security Council.

The recent chairman and a current board member is Stephen Hadley, a principal of Rice, Hadley, Gates, Manuel, a strategic consulting firm. Hadley was the White House foreign policy advisor to President George W. Bush, and directed the National Security Council staff. Condoleezza Rice was Secretary of State and National Security Advisor to G.W. Bush. Robert Gates was Secretary of Defense, Director of Central Intelligence, and National Security Advisor. Anja Manuel served in the Department of State, and is currently on the DoD Defense Policy Board. She is also the Executive Director of the Aspen Strategy Group and Aspen Security Forum, a think-tank.

Vice chair of the USIP is Judy Ansley, a former advisor at the National Security Council. Other board members are Prof. Stephen D. Krasner, also a former NSC member, and Eric S. Edelman, former Undersecretary of Defense for policy. To round out the Board there are some representatives of "civil society" and industry.

One scholar, Michael D. English, author of a critical book on the USIP, reported that:

> [R]etired general Anthony Zinni noted that USIP played a crucial behind the scenes role in "practically every American success in Iraq and Afghanistan," as well as supporting U.S. efforts in democracy promotion and conflict mediation in places such as the Balkans, the Philippines, Somalia and Sudan.[63]

English concluded that:

> The current organization is a reflection of the expansion of the national security state and the pervasive influence of militarism within many sectors of government . . . [rather than] the vision of the peace reformers ... who feel that there is a pressing need for greater examination of how U.S. policy contributes to violent conflict and global instability.[64]

The USIP offers grants to researchers and also convenes Study Groups to provide policy advice to the government. However:

> A secular pattern of USIP funding has been to shun researchers critical of empire, hegemony or U.S. military interventions. There is a veritable unwritten rule at the Institute that endeavours uncovering American foreign policy's underside would never be solicited. . . .[65] Representatives of conservative think-tanks, the State Department and the National Security Council dominate the membership of USIP's Study Groups.[66]

The Institute's extensive worldwide operations are aligned with the U.S. Special Operations Command catalog of "unconventional warfare." For example, the communist revolution in Nepal finally succeeded in 2006, and was in the process of creating a new governing system. The USIP then deemed that Nepal lacked "legal facilities necessary to tackle serious crimes and prevent destabilization."[67] Consequently:

> In April 2008, at the request of Nepal's attorney general, representatives from the [USIP] Rule of Law Center of Innovation returned to Kathmandu to conduct a two-day workshop that focused on human rights and international conventions signed by Nepal; they also examined ways for the post-conflict society to combat serious crimes. A small team in the field worked directly with police and prosecutors. . . .[68]

Training the police! Perhaps the result will be more "peaceful" than a previous covert operation employing Michigan State University professors to train "police" in Vietnam.

In accordance with today's governance pattern of "networking" and "public-private partnerships," the USIP works along with many NGOs in Nepal (international and local, covertly created and grassroots) to protect U.S. political, military, and economic interests. The National Endowment for Democracy funds many of these activities. One of the 4 core institutes of the NED, the Center for International Private Enterprise (CIPE) has as its mission "Strengthening democracy around the globe through private enterprise and market-oriented reforms." CIPE alone has spent millions to tone down the Nepal revolution. It continues to work with youth, through essay contests, workshops and entrepreneurial clubs, hoping to persuade future policymakers that only in a market-based economy can there be democratic freedoms. CIPE partners with:

> Samriddhi, The Prosperity Foundation, among other youth-focused initiatives [that] launched the innovative Arthalaya program, which is a five-day workshop promoting concepts of entrepreneurship and the market economy. The program aims to engage Nepalese youth in the private sector and encourage them to start new businesses and bring new ideas for promoting economic and democratic reform. [69]

Among recent NED-CIPE grants are "Supporting Nepal's Transition Towards a Market-Oriented Federal Democracy" (2018) for $481K[70] and "Investing to Support Nepal's Transition towards a Market Oriented Federal Democracy" (2020) for $873K.[71]

ALBERT EINSTEIN INSTITUTION

The Albert Einstein Institution (AEI), a nongovernmental think tank created by Gene Sharp in 1983, is highly regarded by peace activists as a promoter of non-violent resistance. However, it was an important asset in "color revolutions," regime change operations engineered by the U.S.

> AEI and its offshoots—groups like the Center for Applied Nonviolent Action and Strategies (CANVAS) and the International Center on Nonviolent Conflict (ICNC)—could be found training anti-dictatorship activists around the world.
>
> But not in dictatorial U.S. client states like Chile, Saudi Arabia, El Salvador, and Zaire. In two decades worth of AEI annual reports, there is scarcely mention of these countries.
>
> Rather, AEI and its offshoots emphasize training activists in countries like the Soviet Union, Burma,

Thailand, Tibet, Yugoslavia, China, Cuba, Venezuela, Iran, and post-Soviet Belarus, Ukraine, and Georgia.[72]

How could peace activists support such clear examples of "unconventional warfare" that so obviously violate the non-intervention requirements of the UN Charter? There are several possible explanations. Not only the general public but even many members of the peace movement are unaware of covert actions, as they are laundered through both genuine nongovernmental organizations and U.S. national security "fronts." In the case of the AEI, Michael Barker's 2009 investigation suggested an explanation:

> The problem of elite manipulation of ostensibly progressive groups is not a new problem. However, the overemphasis in Leftist literature on aggressive aspects of imperialism (waged through both overt and covert military, economic, and diplomatic domination) has unfortunately meant that little attention has been paid to the equally important "friendly face" of imperialism that is waged by democracy-manipulating groups like the NED, and liberal foundations (e.g., the Ford Foundation and the Gates Foundation).[73]

Another possible reason for peace activists' silence regarding regime change is a belief, nurtured by the CIA and Special Operations advocates in the military, that considering the high probability of total nuclear destruction in a conventional war, unconventional warfare is a preferred alternative. Assassinating some opponents, overthrowing governments, or propping up unpopular ones may be unsavory, but at least they are unlikely to destroy all human civilization.

Yet another possibility is that some in the peace movement believe that the Cold War designated "evil empires" are the real threat to the continuation of the world, or at any rate, our "freedoms," and therefore any low-intensity warfare to destroy them is justified.

Professor Marcie Smith's research has followed Michael Barker's earlier investigation of AEI.[74] Professor Smith aims to clear the fog, especially for the left and peace activists who continue to admire the AEI, or who know nothing about it. She reports that in 1965, Gene Sharp, while at student at Oxford, was recruited for the Center for International Affairs at Harvard.

> The "CIA at Harvard," as it was then called, was the epi-center of the Cold War intellectual establishment, serving as hearth and home to top-flight Cold Warriors like Henry Kissinger, McGeorge Bundy, Samuel Huntington, and Zbigniew Brzezinski.... [Sharp] was a Cold War defense intellectual.[75]

The AEI continued Sharp's association with the national security establishment, and received funding from the U.S. Institute of Peace, the National Endowment for Democracy, and the International Republican Institute. These agencies also funded the dissidents and regime change groups—"Freedom Fighters"—that AEI was coaching in foreign countries.[76]

Happily, there still are noble anti-war think tanks, for example, the Union of Concerned Scientists, the Center for International Policy, and the Quincy Institute; and also activist NGOs with research divisions such as World Beyond War and CodePink, but their messages aren't loud enough.

University scholars in international relations and related fields are heavily dependent on both funding and contacts from the national security establishment; even the Institute for International Education receives funds from the DoD. In the political science discipline the purveyors of conversion tactics have the greatest distinction: "democratization, i.e., capitalism," "regime change," "counterrevolution." Accordingly, since 1945 "national security" programs in political science have increasingly outshone and attracted students and professors, as opposed to more traditional political science concerns, such as peace, people's power, and the good life. Military and intelligence agency affiliated scholars are the experts, not only training the next generation of students, but those sought after by the media and policy advisory positions in think tanks, industry, and government.

NOTES

The appearance of U.S. Department of Defense (DoD) visual information does not imply or constitute DoD endorsement.

1 Richard M. Abrams. "The U.S. Military and Higher Education: A Brief History," *Annals of the American Academy of Political and Social Science,* Vol. 502 (1989): 15–29.

2 Atomic Heritage Foundation, "University Partners: Manhattan Project History," June 4, 2014, https://www.atomicheritage.org/history/university-partners.

3 David Horowitz, "Sinews of Empire," *Ramparts* (October 1969): 33.

4 Matthew D. Crosston, "Fragile Friendships: Partnerships Between the Academy and Intelligence," *International Journal of Intelligence and CounterIntelligence* 31:1 (2018): 139–58.

5 Lutz, "A Military History of the American Suburbs, the Discipline of Economics, and All Things Ordinary," *Antipode,* Vol. 43, No. 3 (2010): 901.

6 Roberto J. González, "The Rise and Fall of the Human Terrain System," *Counterpunch,* June 29, 2015, https://www.counterpunch.org/2015/06/29/the-rise-and-fall-of-the-human-terrainsystem/

7 David H. Price, *Weaponizing Anthropology* (Petrolia: Counterpunch, 2011), 31.

8 Caucus for a Critical Political Science, https://connect.apsanet.org/s27/. I did follow through on the examination of foundations in Joan Roelofs, *Foundations and Public Policy: The Mask of Pluralism* (Albany: SUNY Press, 2003).

9 Union of Concerned Scientists, "About: History," https://www.ucsusa.org/about/history.

10 Vera Kistiakowsky, "Military Funding of University Research," *The Annals of the American Academy of Political and Social Science 502, Universities and the Military* (March 1989): 153.

11 Ibid.: 148

12 Author's document.

13 Joan Roelofs, *Foundations and Public Policy.*

14 Maryum Elnasseh, "Social Work Students Decry SSA's New Name After Crown Family Donation," *In These Times,* July 20, 2021, https://inthesetimes.com/article/uchicago-military-industrial-complex.

15 U.S. Army, Careers and Jobs: Army ROTC Programs: Find Schools and Military Colleges, https://www.goarmy.com/careers-and-jobs/find-your-path/army-officers/rotc/find-schools.MA-.results.html#s.

16 William M. Arkin and Alexa O'Brien, "The Most Militarized Universities in America: A VICE News Investigation," *VICE News,* November 6, 2015, https://www.vice.com/en/article/j59g5b/the-most-militarized-universities-in-america-a-vice-news-investigation.

17 Ibid.

18 "On December 21, 2019, ICCAE transitioned from the Defense Intelligence Agency (DIA) to the Intelligence Community Human Capital Office (ICHCO), Office of the Director of National Intelligence (ODNI)." Intelligence Community Centers for Academic Excellence, ODNI, https://www.dni.gov/index.php/iccae.

19 Areas of study as determined by the Office of the Director of National Intelligence [https://www.dni.gov/files/CHCO/documents/CAE/ICCAE_FAQs.pdf]: Intelligence/National Security Related Curricula: History and U.S. Intelligence

and National Security; The U.S. Intelligence Community; Intelligence Cycle; Intelligence Collections; Critical Thinking Skills for Intelligence Analysis; Analytic Writing and Briefing; Introduction to Structured Analytic Techniques; Critical Technology History & The Intelligence Community; Artificial Intelligence; Machine Learning; Data Visualization; Computational Statistics/Algorithm Design; Computer Science Analytic Writing and Briefing; STEM: Biosciences, Chemistry, Cognitive Neural and Behavioral Sciences, Computer and Computational Sciences (includes Algorithm Design, Artificial Intelligence, Computational Modeling Techniques, Computational Statistics; Computer Visioning and Machine Learning), Engineering (includes Aeronautical and Astronautical, Chemical, Civil, Electrical, Materials Science, Mechanical and Nuclear), Geosciences, Mathematical Sciences, Oceanography, Physics, Technology, etc.; Language Studies: Arabic; Azerbaijani; Bangla; Burmesel; Cambodian/Khmer; Chinese; Dari; Farsi; French; Georgian; German; Haitian; Kurdish; Lao; Pashto; Persian; Punjabi; Russian; Hindi; Japanese; Indonesian; Korean; Spanish; Swahili; Turkish; Turkmen; Urdu; Uzbek; Vietnamese. https://www.dni.gov/files/CHCO/documents/CAE/ICCAE_FAQs.pdf

20 Matthew D. Crosston, "Fragile Friendships: Partnerships Between the Academy and Intelligence," *International Journal of Intelligence and CounterIntelligence* 31:1 (2018): 139–58.

21 Ibid.

22 Ibid.

23 Henry Giroux, "The Politics of Higher Education and the Militarized Academy after 9/11," *Alif: Journal of Comparative Poetics, No. 29, The University & Its Discontents: Egyptian & Global Perspectives* (2009): 104–126.

24 U.S. Department of Defense, Basic Research/Research Directorate, "DEPSCoR: Defense Established Programs to Stimulate Competitive Research," https://basicresearch.defense.gov/Pilots/DEPSCoR-Defense-Established-Program-to-Stimulate-Competitive-Research/.

25 DARPA is illuminated in Annie Jacobson, *The Pentagon's Brain: An Uncensored History of DARPA, America's Top-Secret Military Research Agency* (New York: Little Brown and Company, 2015).

26 Defense Advanced Research Projects Agency, "About DARPA," https://www.darpa.mil/about-us/about-darpa.

27 Defense Advanced Research Projects Agency, "Six Paths to the Nonsurgical Future of Brain-Machine Interfaces," May 20, 2019, https://www.darpa.mil/news-events/2019-05-20.

28 DARPA Facebook Page (September 17, 2020), https://www.facebook.com/67150982149/photos/a.67177297149/10159137052857150/.

29 DARPA Facebook Page (November 10, 2020), https://www.facebook.com/67150982149/photos/.pb.100064459283250.2207520000../10159286194622150/?type=3

30 U.S. Army Combat Capabilities Development Command Chemical Biological Center, *Cyborg Soldier 2050: Human/Machine Fusion and the Implications for the Future of the DoD* (2019), https://community.apan.org/wg/tradoc-g2/mad-scientist/m/articles-of-interest/300458.

31 Defense Advanced Research Projects Agency, "DARPA Launches Social Media Platform to Accelerate R&D: Social networking collaboration site aims to speed science and tech discovery," March 19, 2019, https://www.darpa.mil/news-events/2019-03-19.

32 Kathryn A. Johnson, "Developing and Signaling Trust in Synthetic Autonomous Agents (SAAs)," U.S. Department of Defense, Defense Technical Information Center, September 26, 2019, https://apps.dtic.mil/sti/citations/AD1099109.

33 Minerva Research Institute, https://minerva.defense.gov/.

34 "Human Geography, Indigenous Mapping, and the U.S. Military: A Response to Kelly and Others' 'From Cognitive Maps to Transparent Static Web Maps'" *Cartographica: The International Journal for Geographic Information and Geovisualization,* Vol. 54, No. 4 (Winter 2019): 288–96.

35 Richard S. Maltz, *Minerva Initiative Conference Report,* September 16, 2010, *Academia,* https://www.academia.edu/32435399/Minerva_Initiative_Conf_Rpt_Maltz_16Sep?email_work_card=view-paper

36 National Academies of Sciences, Engineering, and Medicine, *Evaluation of the Minerva Research Initiative* (Washington, DC: The National Academies Press, 2020), https://www.nap.edu/catalog/25482/evaluation-of-the-minerva-research-initiative.

37 Ibid.

38 Ibid.

39 Catherine Lutz, "The Perils of Pentagon Funding for Anthropology and the Other Social Sciences," *The Minerva Controversy,* The Social Science Research Council, November 6, 2008, http://essays.ssrc.org/minerva/2008/11/06/lutz/

40 Ronald R. Krebs, "Striking the Right Balance: of High Walls and Divisions of Labor," *Perspectives on Politics,* Vol. 8, No. 4 (December 2010): 1113–16.

41 Catherine Lutz, "The Perils of Pentagon Funding for Anthropology and the Other Social Sciences."

42 Dr. J. Christopher Daniel, Senior Advisor for Global Health Engagement to the Assistant Secretary of Defense for Health Affairs, "DoD Global Health Engagement: The Strategic Perspective" (slideshow presented November 2016), slide 16, https://slideplayer.com/slide/14003705/

43 *USASpending.gov,* "About," https://www.usaspending.gov/about: "USASpending.gov is the official source for spending data for the U.S. Government. Its mission is to show the American public what the federal government spends every year and how it spends the money. You can follow the money from the Congressional appropriations to the federal agencies and down to local communities and businesses."

44 Matt Kennard and Mark Curtis, "Key Assange Prosecution Witness Part of Academic Cluster That Has Received Millions from UK & U.S. Militaries," *Declassified UK,* October 2, 2020, https://declassifieduk.org/revealed-key-assange-prosecution-witness-is-part-of-academic-cluster-which-has-received-millions-of-pounds-from-uk-and-us-militaries/

45 SERDP-ESTCP, https://www.serdp-estcp.org.

46 North Atlantic Treaty Organization (NATO), "Science for Peace and Security," updated November 4, 2021, https://www.nato.int/cps/en/natolive/78209.htm.

47 Public Affairs Regional Centre, Republic of North Macedonia, http://parc.morm.gov.mk/.

48 NATO Centres of Excellence, https://www.act.nato.int/centres-of-excellence.

49 NATO Strategic Communications Center of Excellence, https://stratcomcoe.org/about-us.

50 Una Aleksandra Bērziņa Čerenkova, "The People's Republic of China and the Russian Federation as Strategic Allies," NATO Strategic Communications Center of Excellence, July 9, 2020, https://stratcomcoe.org/publications/the-peoples-republic-of-china-and-the-russian-federation-as-strategic-allies/31.
51 *Political Science Jobs Online journal from the American Political Science Association,* Vol. 9, Issue 11 (November 2020).
52 Laleh Khalili, "Stupid Questions," *London Review of Books,* February 24, 2022, https://www.lrb.co.uk/the-paper/v44/n04/laleh-khalili/stupid-questions.
53 Ben Freeman, Foreign Influence Transparency Initiative, *U.S. Government and Defense Contractor Funding of America's Top 50 Think Tanks* (Washington, D.C.: Center for International Policy, October 2020), https://3ba8a190-62da-4c98-86d2-893079d87083.usrfiles.com/ugd/3ba8a1_318530ca605142e68e653d93b5ad698f.pdf.
54 Ibid.
55 Carnegie Endowment for International Peace, *2016 Annual Report,* https://carnegieendowment.org/about/annualreport/2016.
56 Benjamin N. Gedan and Richard E. Feinberg, "Latin America's Leftists Aren't Who You Think," *Foreign Policy,* January 31, 2022, https://foreignpolicy.com/2022/01/31/latin-americas-leftists-arent-who-you-think/?tpcc=recirc_latest062921.
57 The Aspen Institute, *2021 Impact Report & 2020 Annual Report,* https://www.aspeninstitute.org/impact-report/impactreport2021/2020-contributions/.
58 Ken Silverstein, "Think Tanks in the Tank?" *The Nation* (June 10/17, 2013): 18–22.
59 United States Institute of Peace, "About USIP," https://www.usip.org/about.
60 United States Institute of Peace, "Institutional Partners,"https://www.usipglobalcampus.org/current-partners/.
61 Sreeram Chaulia, "One Step Forward, Two Steps Backward: The United States Institute of Peace," *International Journal of Peace Studies,* Vol. 14, No, 1 (Spring/Summer 2009): 65.
62 Sreeram Chaulia, "One Step Forward," 66.
63 Michael D. English, *The U.S. Institute of Peace: A Critical History* (Boulder, CO: First Forum Press, 2018), 3.
64 Ibid., 10.
65 Sreeram Chaulia, "One Step Forward," 70.
66 Ibid., 68.
67 Aaron M. Cohen, "Nepal Reinvents Itself," *Futurist,* Vol. 42, No. 5 (Sept/Oct 2008):16.
68 Ibid., 16.
69 Center for International Private Enterprise, "Celebrating International Youth Day," *CIPE Blog,* August 13, 2012, https://www.cipe.org/blog/2012/08/13/celebrating-international-youth-day/.
70 National Endowment for Democracy, Regions: Nepal 2018, https://www.ned.org/region/asia/nepal-2018/ (accessed in 2019).
71 National Endowment for Democracy, Regions: Nepal 2020, https://www.ned.org/region/asia/nepal-2020/ (accessed in 2021).
72 Marcie Smith, "Getting Gene Sharp Wrong," *Jacobin* (December 2019), https://www.jacobinmag.com/2019/12/gene-sharp-george-lakey-neoliberal-nonviolence.

73 Michael Barker, "Sharp Reflection Warranted: Nonviolence in the Service of Imperialism," *Swan's Commentary*, June 30, 2008, http://www.swans.com/library/art14/barker01.html.

74 Marcie Smith, "Change Agent: Gene Sharp's Neoliberal Nonviolence (Part One)," *Nonsite #28* (May 10, 2019), https://nonsite.org/change-agent-gene-sharps-neoliberal-nonviolence-part-one/.

75 Marcie Smith, "Getting Gene Sharp Wrong."

76 Ibid.

CHAPTER FIVE

PHILANTHROPY AND NONPROFIT ORGANIZATIONS

Philanthropy is such an important part of our culture, politics, and economy, yet critical examinations of its relevance are very rare, and consideration of its relation to militarization even rarer. There is of course a reason for this: the golden goose must not be touched by scholars, journalists or even progressive activists.

What is commonly called "the third sector" consists of thousands of organizations: philanthropies, arts, civil rights, political reform, educational, religious, and others, that are neither governmental nor profit making businesses. Underpinning all these are the foundations that fund them, along with providing helpful directives about how to be effective and reasonable. Yet this "sector" is not independent of either government or business. Government, including the DoD and its associated departments and agencies (Department of Energy, Veterans Affairs, State, Homeland Security, CIA), awards contracts, grants, and charitable donations, often in significant amounts, to these organizations. Military contractors are also important sources of support for nongovernmental organizations (NGOs), and even a small donation can be an effective silencer with regard to any military activities.

In earlier days, corporate philanthropy would be concentrated on the surrounding community and national policy institutions, such as the Council on Foreign Relations.

However, after the radical protests of the 1960s, corporate foundations followed the lead of the major liberal foundations, Ford, Rockefeller, and Carnegie, and starting funding civil rights, anti-poverty, and progressive reform organizations, such as the Urban Coalition. They selected the groups that advocated needed reforms without threatening the U.S. empire or capitalism. The antiwar movement was not neglected; Physicians for Social Responsibility was funded by the Rockefeller Family Fund.

The "free market" doesn't keep the U.S. economy afloat. Government (federal, state, and local), provides a major stabilizer, as advocated by Keynesian economics. Included in this stimulus are social security and other transfer programs, government purchases, and government subsidized or taxpayer financed industries: education, health care, agriculture, housing, highways, other infrastructure, and conservation, to say nothing of the military, which accounts for more than half of the discretionary part of the national budget.

The "third sector" is also an important prop for the economy. It represents about 6% of the Gross Domestic Product.[1] Of greater significance, it picks up the slack left by market forces, and our privatized and inadequately funded government services, to provide the level of "civilization" expected by many citizens, as well as a degree of help for the unfortunate and dispossessed.

For the business sector the privatization of social services, culture, education, and reform has many advantages. Nongovernmental organizations invest their funds in the corporate economy, and their projects do not have to be authorized by legislatures or voters. NGO staff members do not enjoy civil service protection or free speech rights vis-à-vis either profitmaking or nonprofit corporations. It is perfectly legal for NGOs (as well as for-profit businesses) to dismiss workers because of their political views or activities.

Charitable and progressive NGOs, which receive foundation and corporate funding if they are "pragmatic and reasonable," provide jobs for sons and daughters of the elite who might otherwise be unemployed or disaffected, along with people of any social status who are dissident and potentially dangerous. They help resolve the great threat to capitalism identified by Joseph Schumpeter:

> The capitalist process, . . . eventually decreases the importance of the function by which the capitalist class lives. We have also seen that it tends to wear away protective strata, to break down its own defenses, to disperse the garrisons of its entrenchments. And we have finally seen that capitalism creates a critical frame of mind which, after having destroyed the moral authority of so many other

institutions, in the ends turns against its own; the bourgeois finds to his amazement that the rationalist attitude
does not stop at the credentials of kings and popes but
goes on to attack private property and the whole scheme
of bourgeois values.[2]

The NGO world facilitates interaction between the angry poor and
the t-shirted sons and daughters of millionaires. Community foundations
on the local level also mute criticism of the corporate world. Volunteers
and staff do not want to jeopardize their grants, or those for their neighbor's charity. Military industries are especially generous to NGOs, not
only with cash donations, but also by releasing time for employee volunteers to help out in local charities, civil rights, environmental, and other
organizations. Along with early-pensioned veterans, contractor staff can
afford to serve on local political party committees and those small city
and town councils and boards that are essentially volunteer positions.

DEPARTMENT OF DEFENSE PHILANTHROPY

The DoD itself and related government departments engage in
philanthropy. Certain schools and the following national organizations
are eligible to receive donations of DoD surplus property:

- American National Red Cross
- Armed Services YMCA of the USA
- Big Brothers/Big Sisters of America
- Boys and Girls Clubs of America
- Boy Scouts of America
- Camp Fire, Inc.
- Center for Excellence in Education
- Girl Scouts of the USA
- Little League Baseball, Inc.
- Marine Cadets of America
- National Association for Equal Opportunity in Higher
  Education
- National Civilian Community Corps
- National Ski Patrol System, Inc.
- Naval Sea Cadet Corps
- United Service Organizations, Inc.

- U.S. Olympic Committee
- Young Marines of the Marine Corps, and
- League/Marine Corps League[3]

The Denton Program allows nongovernmental organizations to use extra space on U.S. military cargo aircraft to transport humanitarian assistance materials. The Joint Chiefs of Staff publishes a guide to foreign humanitarian assistance and organizations with which to coordinate military operations.

Examples of Humanitarian Assistance Stakeholders

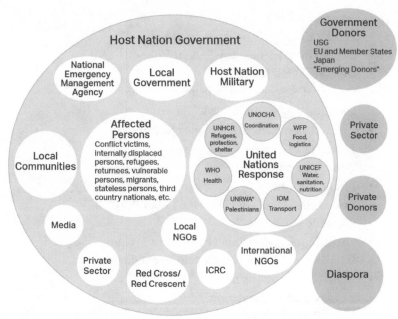

* Present in the Middle East

Legend

EU	European Union	UNOCHA	United Nations Office for the Coordination of Humanitarian Affairs
ICRC	International Committee of the Red Cross		
IOM	International Organization for Migration	UNRWA	United Nations Relief and Works Agency for Palestine Refugees in the Near East
NGO	nongovernmental organization		
UNHCR	United Nations High Commissioner for Refugees	USG	United States Government
		WFP	World Food Program
UNICEF	United Nations Children's Fund	WHO	World Health Organization

Foreign Humanitarian Assistance   Source: DoD

The vast rivers and tributaries of the military establishment have ample funds for good works, along with temporarily underworked personnel. Here are three diverse examples: Oak Ridge National Laboratory (part of the Manhattan Project and still concerned with nuclear weapons production) gives donations to nonprofit organizations promoting STEM education as well as "Community legacy initiatives . . . [Organizations that can] make a positive difference in the overall health and economic vitality of East Tennessee."[4] Political, labor, religious, and sports organizations are not eligible. In October 2021, UT-Battelle, which manages and operates Oak Ridge National Laboratory for the U.S. Department of Energy, announced its grants. These included support for a Free Medical Clinic, and grants to the following:

- American Red Cross
- Blount County Robotics Team 4504
- Catlettsburg Elementary School Robotics
- Celebrate Oak Ridge
- Center of Science and Industry
- Children's Museum of Oak Ridge
- Congressional Medal of Honor Society
- Discover Life in America
- Foothills Land Conservancy
- Friends of Literacy
- Friends of Oak Ridge National Laboratory
- Girls Inc.
- Great Smoky Mountains Institute at Tremont
- International Economic Development Council
- Keep Knoxville Beautiful
- Legacy Parks Foundation
- Little River Watershed Association
- Michael Dunn Center
- Midway Middle School
- Nurture the Next
- Pull for our Veterans
- Shora Foundation
- YWCA
- Zoo Knoxville[5]

UT-Battelle is a private nonprofit contractor, also affiliated with the University of Tennessee. However, its management of Department of Energy and DoD facilities situates it well within the military establishment.

Food Pantry Invitation   Source: DoD National Guard

The Family Food Pantry in Portsmouth, New Hampshire, was generously hosted at the Army National Guard Recruiting Office.

Vandenberg Space Force Base in California is situated on Surf Beach, which also happens to be the habitat of the Western Snowy Plover. To protect this habitat:

> Vandenberg SFB has launched several initiatives aimed at conservation efforts, including establishing a community outreach program. During nesting season, volunteers are tasked with patrolling the beach to ensure nests are preserved and conservation rules are being followed, all while educating beachgoers on the importance of the habitat.[6]

MILITARY-NGO REVOLVING DOORS

There is a "revolving door" between the military and leadership of nonprofit institutions, both board members and top staff. That is not very surprising in the case of national security think tanks and veterans' organizations, but educational institution and citizens' group leaders are also revolvers. Some examples are Robert Gates (Director of Central Intelligence, President of Texas A &M University, Secretary of Defense, President of the Boy Scouts of America, Chancellor of the College of William & Mary); Marsha Johnson Evans (executive director of the Girl Scouts from 1998 to 2002, retired Rear Admiral); and CEO Angie Salinas (Girls Scouts of Southwest Texas, Major General in the United States Marine Corps.)

In recent years, the Carnegie Corporation board of trustees included Condoleezza Rice and General Lloyd Austin III (Ret.), Commander of CENTCOM, a leader in the 2003 invasion of Iraq. He was also a board member of United Technologies and is now Secretary of Defense, despite a tradition of having a civilian in this position. Rear Admiral Harold Bernsen, formerly Commander of the U.S. Middle East Force and not a physician, is a former president of Physicians for Peace (not the similarly named Physicians for Social Responsibility).

HUMANITARIAN AID

Despite its connotations, humanitarian aid is part of "unconventional warfare," according to the U.S. Special Operations Command, reminiscent of the "winning hearts and minds" doctrine. For example, the Navy's hospital ship, *USNS Comfort,* has had a mission at ports in Latin American and the Caribbean. They provided medical and dental care to locals on board and on shore, and veterinarians throughout the countries.[7]

The U.S. European Command Medical Civilian Assistance Program offered medical and dental services in Rwanda and Botswana, publicizing that:

> In one case, a withdrawn elderly man entered the makeshift optometry clinic tent in Rwanda, hunched over nearly crawling so he could see the ground and avoid any obstacles on his way to the exam chair. But he walked out standing tall with a grin from ear to ear.[8]

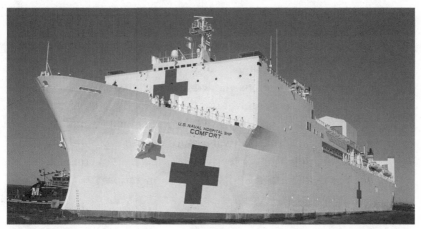

USNS Comfort   Source: DoD Navy

In addition to its own humanitarian work, the DoD funds relief organizations working internationally, for example, the International Rescue Committee, Save the Children, and Mercy Corps. Grantees are expected to be silent about any related military objectives and operations. Sociologist Laura L. Miller has interviewed relief workers serving in Bosnia in 1996 and Haiti in 1997 and found "acceptance and even the advocacy of military intervention on the part of traditionally antimilitary relief workers."[9] She concludes that: "These aid workers have decided that armed intervention in their area of operation is necessary, and they have benefited in other ways from the attention and the assets that accompany the U.S. military."[10] These collaborations have been fruitful, and DoD policy directives urge humanitarian and other NGOs to hire more former military personnel for leadership and staff positions.

FOUNDATIONS

The large liberal foundations, such as Carnegie, Rockefeller, and Sage were from their creation in the early 20th century intent on influencing policy; Ford adopted a national focus in the early 1940s. Along with the Progressive movement, the Ford Foundation wished to remedy the very obvious and self-defeating flaws of capitalism, while retaining the system of corporate power and wealth and its increasing dominance on the world scene. Foundation influence over international, federal, state, and local politics has been enormous, aided by the frequent stagnation of our political institutions, which were not designed to contend with 20th century problems.

> Confronted with the radical protest of the 1960s and 1970s, the foundations funded and nurtured civil rights and anti-poverty organizations that did not threaten corporate dominance, and bypassed the radical anti-capitalist, anti-imperialist and antiwar groups. These were already being disrupted or violently repressed by government, such as by the FBI's COINTELPRO operation.[11]

The foundations argued that they were promoting change that was realistic, and thus supported only those groups they considered "pragmatic." However, the type of organization that met their standards was usually a "single issue" one. This had a strong effect on the dampening of protest, as thousands of tax-exempt nongovernmental organizations were created and existing ones were sustained by foundation grants and technical assistance. Many of the radicals, weary of protesting, were attracted to NGOs with adequate facilities and modern communication systems, while their leaders, tired of being ineffective and repressed, and increasingly encumbered with children and mortgages, could enjoy paid employment, travel allowances, and friendly meetings with political and economic elites. Foundations supported antiwar organizations and supplied a healthy chunk of the peace movement's income.[12]

> The Rockefeller Family Fund, for example, made its first grant, $20,000, to a fledgling organization called Physicians for Social Responsibility in 1979. The money went to hire PSR's first executive director and to open its first office. In 1980 the Fund followed with $33,000 for the executive director's salary and the first test direct mail appeal. It was a classic example of "seed" money at work. PSR took root and flowered. Last year [1982] it reported 100 local chapters, 16,000 members, 30,000 supporters and an annual budget of $500,000. Moreover, its "establishment" credentials undoubtedly created a credibility that sped the growth of concern over the issue.[13]

This was a safe group to inject with funds as "the role of corporate profit–making in the arms race is a concern that receives little emphasis in PSR ... activities."[14]

Favored groups maintain a single issue focus that:

> obscures many of the political and economic underpin-
> nings of militarism. The profit motive leads corporations
> to develop and sell nuclear weapons, nuclear power,
> toxic chemicals, and fossil fuels. Third World nations and
> national minorities in the United States suffer underde-
> velopment and economic exploitation by multinational
> corporations. In support of corporate interests the U.S.
> government intervenes militarily with conventional
> weapons throughout the world, and U.S. military planners
> contemplate the use of theater nuclear weapons in such
> regional conflicts. Yet, from the respectable point of view,
> the complexities and interrelatedness of these issues are
> not a proper concern of the peace movement, since any
> deep analysis would call attention to the profound corpo-
> rate contribution to the risk of nuclear war. Corporations
> and their affiliated philanthropies look favorably on peace
> groups that strictly limit their attention to nuclear war, no
> matter how unrealistic and misleading the single issue
> focus may be.[15]

"Solidarity" groups, such as those that regard Latin American rebellions as the consequence of U.S. military–backed corporations, are not considered "pragmatic." Foundations have countered this perspective by creating Americas Watch, Asia Watch, and similar human rights organizations, as well as funding existing ones such as Amnesty International. These groups contend that the violent and repressive conditions that motivate radicals are primarily caused by a lack of respect for human rights due to untrained local police forces, traditional racism, and patriarchy. The new organizations work to bring human rights violations to the attention of the media and international organizations. Abuses are regarded as "deviations," without connection to foreign corporations or U.S. military training of nationals received at the School of the Americas (now renamed the Western Hemisphere Institute for Security Cooperation) or in their own countries.

NATIONAL ENDOWMENT FOR DEMOCRACY

NGOs are partners, contractors, grantees, and sometimes fronts for government national security departments and agencies. A prime example of the latter relationship is the National Endowment for Democracy, which was created in the wake of revelations in 1967 that the CIA had been covertly funding citizens' organizations via respectable and dummy foundations. The organizations infiltrated included the National Student Association, the American Newspaper Guild, the National Education Association, and the American Federation of State, County and Municipal Employees. Their members (except for top leaders who knew of the CIA arrangement, such as Gloria Steinem of the NSA) were unwitting partners in the Cold War worldwide "unconventional warfare," mostly in attempting to facilitate regime change or propping up governments faced with popular insurrection.

Major liberal foundations have long engaged in covert and overt operations to support imperial projection, described by David Horowitz as the "Sinews of Empire" in his revealing 1969 *Ramparts* article. They have been close associates of the Central Intelligence Agency and were active in its instigation. The Rockefeller and Carnegie foundation-created Council on Foreign Relations has long been a link among Wall Street, large corporations, academia, the media, and our foreign and military policymakers.

> Press reports indicated that the CIA probably had used at least 46 foundations in an involved method of funneling funds to certain organizations. Under a method of transfer known as a "triple pass," the usual procedure was for the CIA to convey funds to "dummy" foundations established by the CIA to act as fronts for its activities. The "dummy" foundations then made grants to legitimate foundations. The legitimate foundations—which also handled other funds—then made grants to certain CIA-designated organizations, using the funds from the "dummy" foundations. . . . A tabulation of press reports shows at least $12,422,925 was channeled to organizations by the CIA.[16]

John J. McCloy, for many years Chairman of the Ford Foundation's trustees, "thought of the Foundation as a quasi-extension of the U.S. government. It was his habit, for instance, to drop by the National Security Council in Washington every couple of months and casually ask whether there were any overseas projects the NSC would like to see funded."[17]

How could the CIA get away with it? All indications suggest that the NGO members were outraged at the *covert nature* of the collaboration. Few objected to the goals of regime change or regime support. This despite their clear violation of international law, as embodied in treaties solemnly ratified by the U.S.: the United Nations Charter and the Charter of the Organization of American States:

> **Article 19, OAS Charter**
> No State or group of States has the right to intervene, directly or indirectly, for any reason whatever, in the internal or external affairs of any other State. The foregoing principle prohibits not only armed force but also any other form of interference or attempted threat against the personality of the State or against its political, economic, and cultural elements.[18]

As a response to the scandal resulting from covert connections to citizen organizations, the National Endowment for Democracy was authorized and funded by Congress—it took until 1983—to do overtly what had been done covertly. It describes itself as an independent nonprofit foundation, but it is undoubtedly a "front." It continues to this day, active in Cuba, Nepal, Venezuela, and elsewhere. Since 2016, the NED has made 334 grants in Ukraine, totaling $22,394,281.[19]

MILITARY CONTRACTOR PHILANTHROPY AND NGOS

Like most businesses, military contractors at one time offered donations mainly to local recreation facilities, the United Way, and national think tanks. Now all types of corporations, often creating their own foundations, provide crucial support for nongovernmental organizations as well as major programs in public schools and universities. Military contractors are awash in funds for philanthropy. This includes not only cash donations but also the creation of joint programs, matching their workers' contributions, and supporting high levels of employee volunteerism.

Contractor benevolence reaches and silences citizens of many interests. There are unsurprising grants to policy-planning think tanks, such as the Council on Foreign Relations, Carnegie Endowment for International Peace, Hudson Institute, Heritage Foundation, Aspen Institute, and the American Enterprise Institute. Military corporations give scholarship aid to aspiring engineers, who may then be predisposed to seek future employment with the benefactor.

However, military contractor philanthropy also endows a large cohort that might otherwise be inclined to antiwar activism. It funds arts organizations and museums, including the JFK Center for the Performing Arts, the Chicago Jazz Orchestra, the Gilbert and Sullivan Society of Houston, the New York Public Library, and the Baltimore Shakespeare Festival.[20] The Art Institute of Chicago's associates include Honeywell International and the Crown Family (General Dynamics), a major benefactor that in 2016 established a $2 million endowment for a Professorship in Painting and Drawing.[21] Wolf Trap Foundation for the Performing Arts is partnered with Northrop Grumman for "arts-based strategies to help pre-K and Kindergartners develop science, technology, engineering and math (STEM) skills."[22] Even the Hancock Shaker Village, once home of a decidedly pacifist sect and now a museum, has received military contractor funds.

Who is aware of these funding sources, you might ask? How can people be silenced if they don't know about their secret Santa? The boards, staffs, and other major non-military donors have adequate data concerning where the funding is coming from. The general membership of organizations and donors all have access to this information via the organization's website, annual reports, and news mailings. Audiences and attendees at events can see donors listed in their programs or very obvious placards throughout the venue, and any who view an organization's website can note sponsorships. Is their reaction to protest and seek to distance themselves from funding ultimately derived from the pursuit of war? Or rather do they simply regard the funding as that entity as doing something positive, for a change? Or do they simply fail to think about it at all?

Furthermore, contractor philanthropy gains much whitewashing publicity by frequently winning awards. In *Corporate Responsibility*

Magazine's 2016 "100 Best Corporate Citizens List," Lockheed Martin was in the top ten, at number 8. Points of Light's 2014 list of the "Civic 50," the Most Community-Minded Companies in America, included General Electric and Raytheon. In March 2016, Bechtel received the U.S. President's Volunteer Services Bronze Award for contributing more than 5,000 volunteer hours in support of Junior Achievement programs. In 2017, the Hispanic Association on Corporate Responsibility recognized 34 Young Hispanic Corporate Achievers; 3 were executives in the weapons industry. Elizabeth Amato, an executive at United Technologies, received the YWCA Women Achievers Award.

Civil liberties and human rights organizations also receive grants: Lockheed gives to the Lawyers Committee for Human Rights, General Electric to the American Civil Liberties Union.

Connections and revolving doors between contractors and NGO boards and top staff further cement bonds and promote a non-critical atmosphere towards U.S. wars and its military industrial complex. In 2002, Chris Hansen, former chief lobbyist for Boeing, became the top lobbyist for the AARP. John H. Biggs was a director of Boeing while he was Chairman, President and CEO of TIAA-CREF, the college teachers' retirement fund. Michele Malone was a leader of National Association for the Advancement of Colored People (NAACP) when an executive at Lockheed.

The NAACP has always had strong connections with major corporations. The civil rights movement of the 1960s prompted new links between activist organizations and business. The Urban Coalition was then created, fostered by the liberal foundations, and thereafter corporate philanthropy became more focused on defusing systemic threats. Its goal was to challenge segregation and discrimination while discouraging the more radical orientations of that era's activists. Lockheed, General Electric (GE), and Boeing became important funders of the NAACP.

Military contractors have donated to every kind of minority organization: Asians Against Domestic Abuse and Vietnamese American Community (Halliburton); American Indian Science and Engineering Society and National Society of Black Engineers (Northrop Grumman); the Holocaust Museum and the Chinese Community Center (GE). Boeing has funded the Congressional Black Caucus and the Urban League. Lockheed has contributed to the Sons of Norway, perhaps to deflect them from the socialistic policies of their homeland. Religious groups of every sect are grantees, not excluding the Benedictine Sisters and Zoroastrians.

Women's organizations are well endowed. Boeing and BAE Systems (the major contractor in New Hampshire) sponsor an American Association of University Women (AAUW) program encouraging females to enter science and engineering. The AAUW's National Tech Savvy Program encourages girls to enter STEM careers, with sponsorship from Lockheed, BAE Systems, and Boeing. GE gives to the Center for Reproductive Law and Policy; Boeing to the National Women's Political Caucus, Lockheed to the National Museum of Women.

Children are nurtured by organizations swaddled in contractor funding. Boy Scouts, Girl Scouts, Boys and Girls Clubs, YMCAs, YWCAs, Little Leagues, UNICEF, and Children's Defense Fund receive substantial grants. Junior Achievement, sponsored by Bechtel, United Technologies, and others, aims to train children in market-based economics and entrepreneurship.

Boy Scouts has been a steady and favored grantee of arms producers. In 2013 Lockheed suspended its donations because of the organization's anti-gay policy, but they are now again among its funders.[23] Corporations are likely to give to their local Boy Scout Council, while staying away from the deeply troubled national organization.

National Guard at Boy Scout Jamboree   Source: DoD National Guard

Girl Scouts has a partnership with Lockheed Martin, among other corporations. Lockheed was a major sponsor of the Girl Scout 2005 National Council Convention and the organization's special program: The Lockheed Martin Science Career Exploration Fund. Tree Musketeers is a national youth environmental organization partnered by Northrop Grumman and Boeing. For all children, Raytheon has provided a simulator, Sum of All Thrills, to allow Walt Disney World visitors to design a virtual reality.

Organizations aiding ill and disadvantaged children such as Child Abuse Network, Children's Brain Tumor Foundation, Make A Wish, Juvenile Diabetes, Special Olympics, and Big Brothers Big Sisters, are also contractor beneficiaries. The board members and staff in such heartbreaking fields, and the parents involved, rarely hesitate to take help from any source.

Military contractors do not neglect health and environmental organizations. The American Lung Association, Canine Companions, Recording for the Blind and Dyslexic, American Cancer Society, and AIDs services indicate the broad range of their largesse.

Clean Air Campaign, Audubon Society, The Nature Conservancy, and the Brooklyn Botanic Garden are among the many environmental organizations receiving contractor donations. A recent trend is "greenwashing" by means of partnerships. Boeing partners with TreePeople to encourage eco-friendly behavior for a healthier and more sustainable Los Angeles, and its Green Teams lead local conservation efforts in the Puget Sound region.[24] The Bechtel Foundation has two programs for a "sustainable California"—an education program to help "young people develop the knowledge, skills, and character to explore and understand the world," and an environmental program to promote the "management, stewardship and conservation for the state's natural resources."[25] With lavish funds it is easy enough to create a local environmental organization and to enlist an energetic teenager to be the "founder" of it.

Lockheed was a sponsor of the U.S. Chamber of Commerce Foundation Sustainability Forum in 2013 and was one of three finalists for the CoC's best Environmental Stewardship Program. Northrop Grumman supports Keep America Beautiful, National Public Lands Day, and partners with the Conservation International and the Arbor Day Foundation forest restoration programs.

United Technologies is the founding sponsor of U.S. Green Building Council Center for Green Schools, a sponsor of the Mayors' Institute for City Design, and co-creator of the Sustainable Cities Design Academy. In 2015, for its efforts in response to climate change, it was awarded a position on the Climate A list of the Climate Disclosure Project. In 2014, Raytheon was "recognized by *Newsweek* as one of America's greenest companies."[26] Pratt and Whitney, a division of United Technologies, produces engines for the Air Force F-16, F-22 and F-35. In October 2015, its employees volunteered to clean up the Connecticut River, which hosts the Electric Boat (a.k.a. nuclear submarine) Company, a division of General Dynamics.

Military contractor philanthropy serves more than merely to improve public relations and silence the boards, staffs, donors, clients, and patrons of recipient NGOs; it enables corporations to shape the content of culture, especially that of youth and minorities, in tune with the values of militarism, notably via organizations such as Boy Scouts, Girl Scouts, the American Association of University Women as well as via the public education system, private schools, colleges, and universities. Thus, our grinding federal taxes, which have reduced local school taxing capacity, are now re-routed through the super profits of the contractors, especially to schools in poor and minority districts. Instead of democratically determined curricula, programs, and scholarships, the MIC does it their way.

Board members and CEOs of the major weapons corporations are also serve on the boards of many nonprofits. To indicate the scope, these include the National Fish and Wildlife Foundation, New York Public Library, Carnegie Hall Society, Conservation International, Wolf Trap Foundation, WGBH (Boston's public TV channel), Boy Scouts, Newport Festival Foundation, Toys for Tots, STEM organizations, Catalyst, the National Science Center, and the U.S. Institute of Peace, along with foundations and universities.

VETERANS' NONGOVERNMENTAL ORGANIZATIONS

Organizations of veterans are legion. "There are more than 45,000 military and veteran non-profits in the United States,"[27] doubtless attesting to our many wars. Some offer social services for all, such as the Pat Tillman Foundation, others provide services to wounded veterans, such as the Air Warrior Courage Foundation, and some support military families, such as the Green Beret Foundation and Our Military Kids, which:

> provides substantial support in the form of grants to the children of National Guard and Military Reserve personnel who are currently deployed overseas, as well as the children of Wounded Warriors in all branches. The grants pay for participation in extracurricular activities and tutoring programs that nurture and sustain children while a parent is away in service to our country or recovering from injury.[28]

Many provide training for civilian careers. The Armed Services Arts Partnership's

> Comedy Bootcamp™ is the first-ever stand-up comedy class designed exclusively for the military community.... Our 600 graduates have gone on to perform for 150,000+ audience members on some of the world's biggest stages, including Warner Theater, Gotham Comedy Club, and The White House.[29]

Comedy Bootcamp   Source: DoD Defense Visual Info

All indications are that this type of training is invaluable for a political career.

Among the veterans' organizations are many that actively seek to influence public policy and political culture. Seven-hundred fifty retired admirals, generals, and other top military leaders are members of Mission: Readiness.

> [They] recognize that the strength of our country depends on a strong military. Since 2009, Mission: Readiness has championed evidence-based, bipartisan state and federal public policy solutions that are proven to prepare our youth for life and to be able to serve their nation in any way they choose.[30]
>
> This is a significant challenge since *71 percent of today's young adults ages 17 to 24 cannot qualify for military service because they are not academically prepared, are too overweight, or have a record of crime or drug abuse.* [Italics added]

What our members fight for:
- High-quality early childhood experiences, including parent coaching and early education, to build a foundation for long-term success
- Nutritious foods and physical activity in schools and communities so children are healthy and physically fit for life
- Strong academic standards that ensure that all students have the opportunity to master the skills and knowledge necessary for postsecondary education, and the option for military service.[31]

NGO INVESTMENT POLICIES

"Socially responsible investing" (SRI) gained currency in the 1960s, although foundations and NGOs rarely followed through on the practice. Those few that attempted this generally used "screens" for investment, commonly avoiding corporations dealing in alcohol, gambling, pornography, and tobacco. Military and weapons firms did not appear in most.

By 2006, environmental, social, and governance (ESG) criteria started to replace SRI in organization investment policies. ESG policies tend to avoid screening out "sin stocks," although they are likely to avoid corporations responsible for excessive carbon emissions. On the other hand, the emphasis on governance led to favoring investments in women or minority owned firms, regardless of what they produce, and count positively toward their mandate.

Commonfund, an asset management company for nongovernmental organizations, produces surveys of the sector's investment policies. Its 2012 study of charities, social service, and cultural organizations reported that 70% of their sample did not consider ESG in their investment policies. Although 61% of religious organizations did employ ESG criteria, merely 16% of social service organizations and 3% of cultural organizations did.[32] In 2021, Commonfund reported that only about 20% of foundations required either ESG or SRI in their investments.[33]

The Interfaith Center on Corporate Responsibility (ICCR) was created by the United Church of Christ in 1971 and it provided major assistance and information for organizations that wanted to engage in SRI. By 2021 the ICCR listed its major issues as Corporate Lobbying & Political Spending, Health Equity, The Climate Crisis and a Just Transition, Food Justice, Human Rights/Worker Rights, Water Stewardship, and Investor Response to the Covid Crisis.[34]

The focus of even the most committed SRI investors—generally churches—has changed, yet the MIC and weapons of mass destruction (WMD) producers are rarely targeted. The United Church of Christ currently offers these advisory guidelines for ESG:

> The Investment Committee has decided that companies in the tobacco, gambling industries, companies that derive a significant portion of their potential emissions, based on proven reserves, from the extraction of thermal coal or oil from tar sands, and domestic companies that are engaged in the production of small arms ammunition or firearms should be avoided to the extent possible within the above policy. In its selection process, the investment manager should avoid securities of companies which derive a significant portion (as defined below) of their business

from the manufacture, sale or distribution of products or
services in these industries.[35]

Most NGOs follow policies similar to that of the Art Institute of
Chicago. In response to a few dissenters, it issued an investment directive in 2013:

> [A]long with the fiduciary responsibility to maxi-
> mize returns on investment consistent with appropriate
> levels of risk, the Art Institute maintains a strong pre-
> sumption against divesting for social, moral, or political
> reasons. This presumption may be overcome only in rare
> and extraordinary circumstances, where the activities
> of the company in question are in direct and significant
> conflict with a core value of the Art Institute or with the
> Art Institute's very mission.[36]

Many nonprofit institutions (as well as individuals and pension
funds) do not have the desire or capacity to create and update investment portfolios. They subscribe to mutual fund offerings of financial
companies such as State Street, Vanguard, BlackRock, Fidelity, College
Retirement Equities Fund (CREF), and others, which are loaded with
military industries: weapons producers, information technology firms,
and other major DoD contractors.[37] Although these funds enable some
invisibility so that the average members, clients or patrons of the NGO
may not be aware of what is in its portfolio, they can easily find out.
The board, staff and major donors surely know the source of the organization's donations. In addition, antiwar organizations such as World
Beyond War produce handy guides to the funds and their military
holdings.[38] Divestment projects of antiwar organizations have the great
merit of informing NGO supporters, pension fund beneficiaries, and the
general public about the major role of military industry in our economy
and culture.

So why do they do it? "Sin" industries have always been among the
most lucrative—guns and drugs—and weapons are a shining example.
Governments can always find a way to afford them and even "neutral"
nations such as Switzerland and Finland want the latest equipment such
as F-35 fighter planes, irrespective of their flaws. Besides, alternative

investments that bring a substantial return and are also "clean" and "safe" are rare. Junk food has fat yields, organic food lean. There have been lone voices that urge the nationalization of the war industries, which would preclude private investment, but that is bucking the trend, as privatization is on the elites' agenda. The collaboration with the military by charities, reformers, artists, musicians, academics, and their organizations will be hard to untangle without addressing the military industrial complex as a whole.

NOTES

The appearance of U.S. Department of Defense (DoD) visual information does not imply or constitute DoD endorsement.

1   Independent Sector 2021, *Health of the U.S. Nonprofit Sector,* https://independentsector.org/nonprofithealth/.
2   Joseph Schumpeter, *Capitalism, Socialism, and Democracy* (New York: Harper and Brothers, 1950), 143.
3   U.S. General Services Administration, Buying and Selling: Eligible Organizations and Activities, https://www.gsa.gov/buying-selling/government-property-for-sale-or-disposal/personal-property-for-reuse-sale/for-state-agencies-and-public-orgs/eligible-organizations-and-activities.
4   Oak Ridge National Laboratory (ORNL), "Grant Opportunities for 501(c)(3) Organizations," https://www.ornl.gov/file/ornlgrantapplicationfinal/display.
5   Oak Ridge National Laboratory, "Area nonprofits receive $150,000 in grants from UT-Battelle," *News Wise,* October 28, 2021, https://www.newswise.com/doescience/area-nonprofits-receive-150-000-in-grants-from-ut-battelle/?article_id=759832.
6   *America's Defense Communities: Resilient Together* (November 2021), Association of Defense Communities, https://defensecommunities.org/wp-content/uploads/2021/10/Americas-Defense-Communities-Magazine-2021.pdf.
7   "Fitzwilliam Navy Lieutenant Aids Underprivileged Throughout Latin America and Caribbean," *Monadnock Shopper News* (July 8–July 14, 2009): 6.
8   Tech. Sgt. Devin L. Fisher, USAF, "Medical Team Examines, Treats Nearly 1,500 African Patients," *Military News,* January 6, 2007, https://military-online.blogspot.com/2007_01_06_archive.html.
9   Laura L. Miller, "From Adversaries to Allies: Relief Workers' Attitudes Toward the U.S. Military," *Qualitative Sociology,* Vol. 22, No. 3 (1999): 196.
10 Ibid.: 181.
11 Federal Bureau of Investigation, "COINTELPRO," *FBI Records: The Vault,* https://vault.fbi.gov/cointel-pro.
12 Kathleen Teltsch, "Filling Big Hopes with Small Grants," *New York Times* (1 May 1985): C1.
13 Susan Reed, "Nuclear Anonymity," *Foundation News* (January/February 1983): 42–49.

14 Talmadge Wright, Feliz Rodrigues, and Howard Waitzkin, "Corporate Interests, Philanthropies, and the Peace Movement," *Monthly Review* (February 1985): 19–31.

15 Ibid.

16 "On CIA Disclosures," *Congressional Quarterly* (Feb. 24, 1967): 271.

17 Kai Bird, *John J. McCloy and the Making of the American Establishment* (New York: Simon & Schuster, 1992), 519.

18 Organization of American States, Department of International Law (DIL), *Charter of the Organization of American States* (a-41), https://www.oas.org/en/sla/dil/inter_american_treaties_A-41_charter_OAS.asp#Chapter_II.

19 National Endowment for Democracy's searchable grants database (accessed February 2022), https://www.ned.org/wp-content/themes/ned/search/grant-search.php.

20 Information for grants and other support is based on annual reports of both contractors and organizations, tax forms online, and information from *Guidestar.org* and similar databases.

21 "SAIC Receives $2 Million Gift from the Crown Family," *School of the Art Institute of Chicago,* https://www.saic.edu/press/saic-receives-2-million-gift-crown-family.

22 Wolf Trap Institute, "Wolf Trap & Northrop Grumman: Partners in STEM Learning Through the Arts," *All Access,* https://allaccess.wolftrap.org/2016/01/07/wolf-trap-northrop-grumman-partners-in-stem-learning-through-the-arts/.

23 Nelson Garcia, "Boy Scouts send 'STEM in a Box' to schools," *9News,* June 2, 2021, https://www.9news.com/article/news/education/stem-school-kits-pandemic/73-9d0ccd55-b805-43d6-b00d-5f4f1ebf04cb.

24 TreePeople, https://www.treepeople.org/.

25 S. D. Bechtel, Jr. Foundation, http://sdbjrfoundation.org/the-foundation/.

26 Newsweek Green Rankings: World's Greenest Companies 2014, *Newsweek,* June 4, 2014, https://www.newsweek.com/green/worlds-greenest-companies-2014.

27 Veterans Advantage, "Organizations Doing Good for Veterans and Their Families," https://www.veteransadvantage.com/giving-back/trusted-military-organizations-and-nonprofits#:~:text=Organizations%20Doing%20Good%20for%20Veterans,profits%20in%20the%20United%20States

28 Charity Navigator rating profile for Our Military Kids, https://www.charitynavigator.org/index.cfm?bay=search.summary&orgid=12532&oldpage

29 Armed Services Arts Partnership, "Comedy Bootcamp," https://asapasap.org/comedy/.

30 Mission: Readiness, Council for a Strong America, https://www.strongnation.org/missionreadiness

31 Mission: Readiness, Council for a Strong America, "About Us," https://www.strongnation.org/missionreadiness/about-us

32 Commonfund Benchmarks Study, Operating Charities Report FY 2013, https://www.commonfund.org.

33 Commonfund, "Viewpoint | The Climate for Responsible Investing is Changing," September 22, 2021, https://www.commonfund.org/research-center/articles/the-climate-for-responsible-investing-is-changing.

34 Interfaith Center on Corporate Responsibility, "ICCR's Issues," https://www.iccr.org/iccrs-issues.

35 The Pension Boards—United Church of Christ Statement of Investment Policy
     (July 2019): 23. https://www.pbucc.org/images/pbucc/investments/PB_IPS.pdf.
36 Dustin Lowman, "Divestment, Part 2: A 'Neutral' Policy," *f newsmagazine,*
     November 22, 2019, https://fnewsmagazine.com/2019/11/divestment-part-2-a-
     neutral-policy/
37 List of investment funds' military holdings, World Beyond War, November 2016,
     https://worldbeyondwar.org/wp-content/uploads/2016/11/indirect.pdf.
38 Ibid.

CHAPTER SIX

STATE AND LOCAL GOVERNMENTS

MILITARY DEPARTMENTS

Most state governments (and territories) have military departments, sometimes called Department of Military and Veterans Affairs; a few states perform such functions in the Office of Adjutant General. In all, their prime responsibility is the management of the National Guard, which may have Army, Air Force, and/or Navy units. The Guard's pay is funded by the state, or by the DoD when called into national service.

However, DoD funding for infrastructure is considerable. For example, for the period 2015–2017, New Hampshire received $18m. for "National Guard Military Operations and Maintenance Projects."[1] These included real property maintenance, electronic security system installation, range maintenance, distance learning centers, environmental compliance/corrective projects, natural and cultural resource management, painting aircraft, and state family program activities. A variety of business and nonprofit service providers benefit from these expenditures.

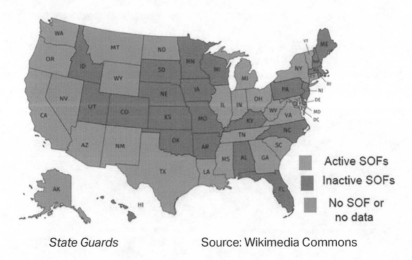

Active SOFs

Inactive SOFs

No SOF or no data

State Guards   Source: Wikimedia Commons

Twenty-two states also have State Guards, which have duties for emergency management and homeland security and may have Army, Navy, or Air Force units. In Ohio there is a Cyber Reserve commanded by the Adjutant General, engaging civilian volunteers who assist local governments with cybersecurity. They also "assist STEM teachers by providing mentors for high school cyber clubs."[2] The State Guards, unlike the National Guards, cannot be called into federal government services. They are like "fall back" armies, able to serve state needs when the National Guards are federalized.

The Washington State Military Department includes the Washington Youth Academy, which bills itself as providing "a highly disciplined, safe and professional learning environment that empowers at-risk youth to improve their educational levels and employment potential and become responsible and productive citizens of the State of Washington."[3] Each youth must find a mentor, and the suggested sources are: "School teachers, counselors, coaches, JROTC leaders; Parents' work associates, friends, neighbors; Extended family members-aunts, uncles, and cousins; Community organizations-YMCA, YWCA, Boy and Girls Clubs, Lion's Club, Kiwanis, Rotary, VFW; Religious Organizations-pastor, imam, rabbi."[4] The mentor cannot be the youth's military recruiter.

> The Washington Youth Academy is a National Guard Youth ChalleNGe Program [these exist in 32 states]. Established under authority of both federal and state law, the WYA is a state-run residential and post-residential intervention for youth who have dropped out of high school or are at risk of dropping out. The Washington Youth Academy is a quasi-military training and mentoring program for at-risk youth. The goal of the program is to give youth a second chance to become responsible and productive citizens by helping them improve their life skills, education levels, and employment potential.[5]

Youth Challenge Academy   Source: DoD National Guard

The California Military Department has a string of eight youth academies, for those "at risk of dropping out of high school or credit deficient." Applicants must provide their own mentors from the general public; "Teachers, coaches, counselors, neighbors, family friends, ministers are great sources to start with when looking for a mentor."[6]

The California Military Institute serves those in grades 5–12, and describes itself as:

> a college preparatory school for students who want to get more out of their educational experience, are not afraid to work hard and challenge themselves.... We believe that a well-rounded individual is not someone who is excellent in academics only, but also someone who is a responsible, ethical, moral citizen, a leader in his or her community imbued with a spirit of service. We achieve this by applying the structure and principles of the Junior Reserve Officer Training Corps.[7]

The California Military Department's Youth and Community Programs Task Force also includes the DoD STARBASE program, which exists at 70 U.S. public schools. Students participate in challenging "hands-on, minds-on" activities in Science, Technology, Engineering, and Math (STEM). They interact with military personnel to explore careers and observe STEM applications in the "real world." The program provides students with 25 hours of stimulating experiences at National Guard, Marine, Air Force Reserve, Army, and Air Force bases across the nation. DoD STARBASE's primary focus is the program for fifth graders. The goal is to motivate them to explore STEM opportunities as they continue their education. The academies serve students that are historically underrepresented in STEM: students who live in inner cities or rural locations, those who are socio-economically disadvantaged, low in academic performance, or have a disability are in the target group.[8]

The DoD also has a program in which National Guard forces are partnered with foreign countries, providing another node of networking for the U.S. military. For example, Austria will be the third partner of the Vermont National Guard, along with North Macedonia and Senegal.[9]

COUNCIL OF STATE GOVERNMENTS

The Council of State Governments, a research and lobbying NGO of state officials, has large contracts with the DoD for disaster preparedness planning. It also has several partnerships. One of these has earned the organization at least two grants, totaling $6m., for participation in the Overseas Voting Initiative (OVI).[10]

> OVI helps state policymakers, election officials and other election community stakeholders understand the unique voting challenges faced by uniformed services personnel and other U.S. citizens overseas and helps those stakeholders develop methods for improving the voting process for these individuals.[11]

Another partnership is for developing "New Interstate Compacts for Occupational Licensure Portability." A major goal of the DoD is "to help military spouses and other practitioners gain professional license portability," yet as with the overseas voting provisions, the compacts will assist all people who wish to practice their professions without unnecessary and protectionist restrictions on out-of-state applicants.[12] We can thus observe that whatever may be the intention of the DoD, some of its interventions into civilian life serve to bypass our sluggish political system, and for this the military receives positive recognition.

STATE CIVILIAN DEPARTMENTS

Various states' departments receive contracts or grants from the DoD, for example, those concerned with the environment, transportation, and business. The New Hampshire Department of Business and Economic Affairs has grants from the Defense Logistics Agency to increase the number of businesses that apply for government contracts; one such grant was for $377,000. As is common with many agencies of the DoD, networking helps the collaboration of military and civilian institutions. The Procurement Technical Assistance Centers program works in cooperation with states (also Washington, D.C., Puerto Rico, Guam, and Northern Mariana Islands), local governments, and nonprofit organizations, while the DoD provides most of the funds. It aims at small businesses that are not yet aware of these lucrative opportunities or that don't know how to go about obtaining them. The program, although under the parachute of the DoD, also aids those seeking contracts from other federal agencies, state and local governments, and government prime contractors.[13]

Environmental Departments

Prominent among the DoD-state cooperative activities is the Environmental Restoration Program. "This program seeks to facilitate State and territory participation in expediting cleanup at DoD hazardous waste sites, and to foster relations between States, military services, Defense agencies and DoD."[14] One grant alone for $1.7m went to the New Hampshire Department of Environmental Services. The Navy has an extensive community participation program for environmental restoration, such as the project in Chesapeake, Virginia, below:

Community Involvement Plan
Chesapeake, Virginia
Source: DoD Navy

The DoD has many environmental partnership programs that engage states, local governments, nonprofit organizations, universities, and other federal departments.

> The Strategic Environmental Research and Development Program (SERDP) is DoD's environmental science and technology program, planned and executed in partnership with DOE and EPA, with participation by numerous other federal and non-federal organizations.... The development and application of innovative environmental technologies will reduce the costs, environmental risks, and time required to resolve environmental problems while, at the same time, enhancing and sustaining military readiness.[15]

One of the projects, with cooperators including the State of Hawaii Department of Land and Natural Resources, was "Seed Dispersal Networks and Novel Ecosystem Functioning in Hawaii." The principal researcher was Dr. Jeffrey Foster of Northern Arizona University, and per the final report (University of New Hampshire, July 2019), the problem to be solved was:

> Most native Hawaiian plant species are bird-dispersed, yet no native avian dispersers remain in most Hawaiian ecosystems. Thus, ecosystem functioning will only be maintained by the handful of invasive vertebrate dispersers that now reside on the islands, most of which are birds. In this context, research efforts must shift focus to non-native bird species (and potentially rats) and the potential for these species to maintain native plant communities under current and predicted environmental conditions. To successfully manage and preserve Hawaiian terrestrial ecosystems, it is necessary to identify and characterize non-native invasive species that are dispersers of desired plant species, determine their role in ecosystem function, and improve non-native plant management plans, while facilitating the recovery of native threatened, endangered, and at-risk plants.[16]

Another SERDP project focused on "management implications for forests disrupted by the invasive plant species *Alliaria petiolata* (garlic mustard)."[17] The investigators were Dr. Kristina Stinson of the University of Massachusetts, Amherst and Dr. Serita Frey of the University of New Hampshire, and the stakeholders were: West Point Military Academy, Army Corps of Engineers (Indian Hollow), The Trustees of Reservations, Pittsfield State Forest, Harvard Forest, Black Rock Forest Consortium, Mass Audubon Society-Drumlin Farm, and an anonymous private landowner. The report has no discussion of how this threat might interfere with the mission of our military or why the military should be supporting it. Yet another program:

Garlic Mustard Project   Source: DoD SERDP

The Readiness and Environmental Protection Integration (REPI) Program is a key tool used by DoD and its partners to protect the military's ability to train, test, and operate in the state. DoD created the REPI Program in response to the development of lands and loss of habitat in the vicinity of or affecting its installations, ranges, and airspace that can lead to restrictions or costly and inadequate training and testing alternatives. Through REPI, DoD works with state and local governments, conservation organizations, and willing private landowners to address these challenges to the military mission and the viability of DoD installations and ranges.[18]

REPI projects in Maine include the Navy's Survival, Evasion, Resistance, and Escape (SERE) School that preserves a realistic isolated environment where "sensitive" training can be performed. This may include role-playing demonstrations of techniques for resistance if captured by the enemy. Expenditures for this project as of FY 2020 were $3,683,750 from REPI and $865,250 from partners.[19]

Completed Joint Land Use Studies
120 Completed as of June 2015
(1985-2015)

Programs for Compatible Civilian Use
Source: DoD Office of Economic Adjustment

ARMY CORPS OF ENGINEERS

From its origin at the beginning of our nation, the Army Corps of Engineers (USACE) has constructed both military and civilian works. These included coastal fortifications, mapping the American West, lighthouses, post offices, jetties and piers, and mapping navigation channels. It later engaged in flood control and the creation of hydroelectric energy. Now the Corps is very visible as it constructs and maintains state and national parks and recreation, and its funding is a consistent part of the DoD budget. The Corps' nearly 3,000 recreation sites nationwide are also serviced by contractors. In New Hampshire these include several towns that provide police protection, a county contract for radio dispatch services, and private companies providing janitorial and landscaping services.

Corps personnel, in conjunction with the New Hampshire Department of Natural and Cultural Resources, manage the natural resources at Hopkinton-Everett Lakes. There and throughout the nation, the Corps sponsor a Junior Ranger program:

> The objective of this program is to develop in the young people who visit Corps of Engineers lakes an awareness of the environment and the role the Corps plays in managing this environment at the lakes, and to solicit their assistance in helping Corps rangers in serving the public and protecting our lands and natural resources.[20]

Junior Ranger
Source: U.S. National Park Service

On its other side, the Corps continues to build military facilities in the U.S. and abroad. "During the Cold War, Army engineers managed construction programs for America's allies, including a massive effort in Saudi Arabia."[21]

> Working at USACE as a civilian employee [most workers are civilians] means making a direct contribution to war fighters and their families, supporting overseas contingency operations, developing technology and systems that save the lives of soldiers and civilians, providing disaster relief, and protecting and enhancing the environment and the national economy. Jobs include: Ecology, Fish Biology, Wildlife Biology, Park Ranger, Biologists, Natural Resources Specialists, Engineering Technician, Architects, Environmental Engineers, and Information Technology Management.[22]

One may volunteer for the Corps:

> [I]n recreation and natural resources management on its nearly 12 million acres of land and water ... [and] Serve as a Park or Campground Host, Staff a Visitor Center, Maintain park trails and facilities, Lead tours of the lock, dam or power plant, Present educational programs, Clean shorelines, Restore fish and wildlife habitat.... Volunteers serve without pay, but are often provided with a free RV campsite with hookups. Training, supervision, tools and supplies are provided. Volunteers receive the same benefits and protection as federal employees.[23]

Clearly, the USACE has performed essential and welcome services to our nation. In retrospect, we may question some of the environmental effects of the hydroelectric projects (e.g., TVA, Bonneville Dam); yet a modern industrial nation requires considerable disruption of the natural world. Military needs were also motives for these projects, which provided energy for weapons, at first conventional and eventually, nuclear. A civilian infrastructure and environmental restoration agency with its own budget could do all the good work, undo the ties with the military mission and reroute all the funding that otherwise goes through the military middleman, further militarizing civilian life.

ECONOMIC DEVELOPMENT COMMISSIONS

Economic development commissions exist at every level of government. They are a reminder that although the "free enterprise" advocates claim that it can "do everything better" than government, free enterprise alone can't keep the economy going. The commissions are usually public-private partnerships and are interlinked with the U.S. government Economic Development Administration and the National Association of Development Organizations (NADO). NADO highlights how Connecticut's huge economic recovery from recession was made possible by military spending:

> This boost had much to do with the region's defense industry, centered around General Dynamics Electric Boat and the Naval Submarine Base New London (both located in Groton). An increase in submarine production has led to the creation of 2,000 new Electric Boat jobs in Connecticut just last year. It is expected that Electric Boat will have 13,000 Connecticut-based employees by 2034. Additionally, there is a major opportunity to grow the supply chain businesses that support major defense contractors. "Workforce development is now front and center as an economic development priority for our region, as well as placemaking and housing—the things that make people and their families want to live here," says Cowser. This means tapping into the region's assets, such as cultural, arts and tourism destinations, including two large Native American casinos that are growing and diversifying.[24]

The network includes state agencies such as the Missouri Military Preparedness and Enhancement Commission, MassDevelopment (MA), and regional ones like the Hampton Roads Military and Federal Facilities Alliance (Virginia). The Washington State Department of Commerce boasts:

Tens of thousands of jobs and billions of dollars flow into the state's economy from the military and defense sector. Washington has six active-duty military installations as well as a major homeland security installation, two Department of Energy facilities, and two world-class universities performing defense-related research within its borders.

Washington is 6th in the nation in the number of active-duty military, with 69,125 military personnel and another 90,246 dependents and 19,474 reservists. The military and defense sector employs another 39,000 civilians, mostly at Joint Base Lewis-McChord (JBLM) and Puget Sound Naval Shipyard (PSNS).

Washington is vital to U.S. defense policies for many reasons. The state's deep water ports, strategically located airports, proximity to the Pacific Rim and integrated rail and road system, as well as a *pro-military civilian population* [emphasis added], allow the various branches to meet their mission needs with tremendous flexibility and collaboration.[25]

The Washington Economic Development Association is typical of the inclusive agency tying major players together: "WEDA members include economic development organizations, cities, counties, ports, tribes, businesses, education and community-based organizations that prioritize economic development."[26] Not all are willing collaborators. A South Whidbey environmental group protested a state commission's ruling that Navy special forces could conduct clandestine training operations in state parks.[27] The group's efforts have resulted in a 2022 ruling by a county court reversing the decision and banning military training in 28 coastal Washington State Parks.

New Hampshire has plenty of these state, city, county, and regional agencies, and also an Aerospace & Defense Export Consortium. Its members include large weapons corporations (e.g., BAE Systems, Elbit) and small businesses, cities, law firms, insurance agencies, aviation and Navy SEAL museums, banks, our Senators and Representatives, a passenger airport, state colleges and universities, a Catholic university, a public technology high school, consulting firms, and U.S. government departments.[28]

Another type of military-local government network is represented by the Association of Defense Communities:

> We are the connection point for leaders from communities, states, the military and industry on community-military issues by enhancing knowledge, information sharing, and best practices. With nearly 300 communities, states, regions, and affiliated industry organizations, ADC represents every major defense community/state in the nation.[29]

Among the organization's concerns are the needs of military families, such as providing work opportunities for military dependents, and sweeteners for the communities. In 2020, the DoD's Office of Local Defense Community Cooperation issued grants totaling $50m, including $10 million, half the funds, for the Big Sky Recreation Center in Great Falls, Montana.

> It will be the only public indoor pool facility in the area, providing residents of the region a chance to enjoy recreational activities, including swimming—even in the winter. The recreation center will also serve as a training facility for the 40th Helicopter Squadron and the 120th Airlift Wing from Malmstrom Air Force Base.[30]

Other grants funded a makers lab (like a library, only for tools) for a public school in Texas, an early childhood center in Missouri, and a Magic City Discovery Center in Minot, North Dakota.

The ADC recognizes "champions," among them a Garrison Command Sergeant Major at Fort Stewart, Georgia. When the COVID-19 pandemic shut down the local farmers' market, she worked with the local Chamber of Commerce and volunteer soldiers to create a system where people would pay $25 for a box of local produce to be picked up at the Chamber's parking lot.[31]

INVESTMENTS

State and local government general funds and pension funds are heavily invested in weapons manufacturers. We have copious information about these thanks to the volunteer researchers in the World Beyond War-Code Pink divestment project.[32] The California Public Employees Retirement System (CalPERS), the second largest U.S. pension fund, is invested in Lockheed, Boeing, BAE, General Dynamics, Leonardo, Thales and many others. Military contractors other than weapons makers also provide substantial returns, such as information technology consultant Accenture, and construction and logistics companies.

The California State Teachers Retirement System has holdings in the major weapons firms and also in Fluor, a military construction company that usually earns the highest annual DoD funding. North Dakota, the state with a public bank, has placed large investments of its Public Employees Retirement System with weapons producers.

New York state and local employees, including teachers, police, and firefighters' retirement funds are heavily invested in weapons companies, as is the separate New York City Teachers' Retirement System.[33] In December 2021, the New York City Council passed legislation requiring City funds to divest from nuclear weapons producers, reaffirmed the City as a nuclear-weapons free area, and *called upon* public employee pension funds to divest from the nuclear weapon industry. The Council also asked the U.S. government to join the Treaty on the Prohibition of Nuclear Weapons.[34] As of January 2020, the only city funds with divestment requirements were Berkeley, California, San Luis Obispo, California, Charlottesville, Virginia, Santa Monica, California, and West Hollywood, California.[35] The Burlington, Vermont City Council passed a resolution in July 2021 to keep city funds out of weapons manufacturers. It exempted the Burlington Employees' Retirement System from this directive but *requested* that it divest from weapons companies.[36]

These meagre victories of the divestment projects indicate how far there is to go. State and local civil servants have reasons other than their pension funds to be unlikely protestors of the military mission and budget. The economic benefits of military industries and bases ensure robust tax receipts for local governments, protecting jobs and enhancing community services. Furthermore, state governments are military-friendly and expect their civil servants to be so, also:

No one has been prosecuted under the Selective Service Act for decades, but Congress and many state governments have adopted additional sanctions to coerce young men to register. For example, male applicants for federal job training and jobs in federal executive branch agencies must prove that they have registered or that they are exempt, according to the Center on Conscience and War. Many states have adopted similar measures, including requirements that men be registered before receiving a driver's license. In New Hampshire, male non-registrants are barred from state jobs and admission to state-funded institutions of higher education.[37]

MILITARIZATION OF POLICE

The militarization of the police has led to many protests, but these have not been against the weapons themselves, just about who should have them:

> SWAT teams—possessing military dress and armaments such as launchable ballistics, sniper rifles, and armed rescue vehicles—were designed to be used in extraordinary, emergency situations, such as a hostage situations. But with the advent of the war on drugs, followed by the war on terror, money and equipment became increasingly available to law enforcement, leading to an alarming increase in the number of jurisdictions with such specialized units.[38]

It has been estimated that one in three police departments in the U.S. have this equipment, transferred by the DoD and funded by the Department of Homeland Security. School districts, college police, and state park officers are eligible to receive this military surplus. This bounty is known as the 1033 Program, named for its section in the 1997 National Defense Authorization Act.

In 2012, Keene, New Hampshire purchased a Lenco BearCat through this program, with funding of $286,00 from the Department of Homeland Security. "Other towns can use the vehicle by signing an agreement with Keene and paying $100 a year, but the BearCat can

Disposal of Surplus Military Equipment
Source: DoD Defense Logistics Agency

Bearcat
Source: Creative Commons

only be driven by Keene police officers."[39] Long Beach, California is replacing their BearCat with a 2022 updated version. DoD surplus accumulates very quickly, to keep the manufacturers going.

A report by The Marshall Project, a nonprofit news organization monitoring the criminal justice system, points out:

> The debate over the militarization of America's police has focused on the accumulation of war-grade vehicles and artillery and the spread of paramilitary SWAT teams. What has gone largely unstudied, however, is the impact of military veterans migrating into law enforcement. Even as departments around the country have attempted a cultural transformation from "warriors" to "guardians," one in five police officers is literally a warrior, returned from Afghanistan, Iraq or other assignments.
>
> Today just 6 percent of the population at large has served in the military, but 19 percent of police officers are veterans, . . . the result of laws that require law enforcement agencies to choose veterans over candidates with no military backgrounds.[40]

The Marshall Project report also noted that:

> The Justice Department and the International Association of Chiefs of Police put out a 2009 guide for police departments to help with their recruitment of military veterans. The guide warned: "Sustained operations under combat circumstances may cause returning officers to mistakenly blur the lines between military combat situations and civilian crime situations, resulting in inappropriate decisions and actions—particularly in the use of less lethal or lethal force."[41]

Firefighters and prison personnel are also occupations often filled by veterans. Beyond that, it is common in state and local civil service systems, as in the federal, to give preference to veterans in hiring. This explains much of the silence of government employees' local unions or the American Federation of State, County, and Municipal Employees (AFSCME), once known for its activism as it concerns U.S. wars.

STATE COLLEGES AND UNIVERSITIES

State colleges and universities receive the same copious R&D contracts as the private institutions, but historically their connections to the military have been stronger. Most were funded as land-grant colleges, endowed by the Morrill Act of 1862 granting federal lands to the states. Each state received 30,000 acres of land per each member of its Congressional delegation; Eastern states acquired acreage from the West. The land would be sold, funds invested, and the interest applied:

> [T]o the endowment, support, and maintenance of at least
> one college where the leading object shall be, without ex-
> cluding other scientific and classical studies, and includ-
> ing military tactics, to teach such branches of learning as
> are related to agriculture and the mechanic arts.[42]

An investigative journalism report has documented in great detail that the Morrill acres, about 10.7 million, were taken from "nearly 250 tribes, bands and communities through over 160 violence-backed land cessions, a legal term for the giving up of territory."

Land-grant institutions are required to maintain the Reserve Officers' Training Corps (ROTC) program. During the Vietnam war period some state university faculties voted to end their institutions' ROTC programs, but the students, with their scholarships, and the trustees, with their charters, did not let that happen. The Massachusetts Institute of Technology (MIT), usually receiving the highest annual amount of DoD university contracts, is a rare private land-grant institution.

An investigative journalism report has documented in great detail that the Morrill acres, about 10.7 million, were taken from "nearly 250 tribes, bands and communities through over 160 violence-backed land cessions, a legal term for the giving up of territory."[43]

State universities may also participate in training foreign militaries (see Chapter 2). Virginia Polytechnic Institute and State University (Virginia Tech), a public land grant institution, has a ROTC program, and in addition, it is one of six Senior Military Colleges, equivalent to the Army, Navy, and Air Force Academies, except that cadets study alongside civilian students. Students in both categories will end up serving the military:

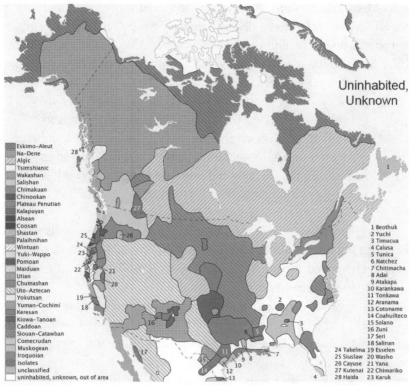

Uninhabited, Unknown

Eskimo-Aleut
Na-Dene
Algic
Tsimshianic
Wakashan
Salishan
Chimakuan
Chinookan
Plateau Penutian
Kalapuyan
Alsean
Coosan
Shastan
Palaihnihan
Wintuan
Yuki-Wappo
Pomoan
Maiduan
Utian
Chumashan
Uto-Aztecan
Yokutsan
Yuman-Cochimí
Keresan
Kiowa-Tanoan
Caddoan
Siouan-Catawban
Comecrudan
Muskogean
Iroquoian
isolates
unclassified
uninhabited, unknown, out of area

1 Beothuk
2 Yuchi
3 Timucua
4 Calusa
5 Tunica
6 Natchez
7 Chitimacha
8 Adai
9 Atakapa
10 Karankawa
11 Tonkawa
12 Aranama
13 Cotoname
14 Coahuilteco
15 Solano
16 Zuni
17 Seri
18 Salinan

24 Takelma 19 Esselen
25 Siuslaw   20 Washo
26 Cayuse   21 Yana
27 Kutenai   22 Chimariko
28 Haida   23 Karuk

Native Language Areas   Source: Wikimedia Commons

Today's national security state includes a growing cadre of technicians and security professionals who sit at computers and manage vast amounts of data; they far outnumber conventional soldiers and spies. And as the skills demanded from these digital warriors have evolved, higher education has evolved with them.[44]

In addition to longstanding ties between the DoD and state universities (and state colleges, community colleges, along with entities such as Virginia Military Institute), these institutions also have many connections to military contractors. They are sometimes revealed in the brave but sporadic protests and resolutions of students. For example, the Divest from the War Machine antiwar website pointed out that "Portland State University School of Business has a partnership with Boeing through its supply chain internship program."[45]

Many scholarships, internships, and joint programs, especially in the STEM subjects, are funded by weapons makers, and this has only intensified with the declining support for higher education in state budgets. BAE Systems has a partnership with the University of New Hampshire:

> [T]he 'BAE Systems Summer STEM Scholar Program' provided scholarships for 10 students to attend the university's Tech Leaders camp. The project was designed and run by seven BAE Systems engineers, who also served as mentors for the students and provided insight on what it is like to have a career at BAE Systems.[46]

Investment of state university funds in the major weapons makers has been publicized through student resolutions, and the work of peace organizations and investigative journalists. Significant investments are also held in private institutions' portfolios.

Military and contractor personnel serve on state institutions' boards of trustees and as university presidents. Before becoming the Secretary of Defense, Robert Gates was Director of the CIA, and then president of Texas A&M University. Among his other connections are service of the boards of Fidelity Funds, the American Council on Education, and the National Association of State Universities and Land-Grant Colleges, and President of the Boy Scouts of America.[47]

SCIENCE, TECHNOLOGY, ENGINEERING AND MATHEMATICS (STEM)

Weapons contractors generously fund all types of educational institutions, taking a particular interest in STEM disciplines. They sponsor in-school programs, field trips, and send tutors to schools. They are sponsors and partners of FIRST, "For Inspiration and Recognition of Science and Technology," a nonprofit that aims to increase interest in STEM education. Among the partners are BAE Systems, Bechtel, Boeing, Booz Allen, Lockheed, and United Technologies.

FIRST is a public-private partnership. In New Hampshire, that includes BAE Systems, the DoD; and the New Hampshire Department of Education, which gives grants to every public and charter school in New Hampshire so that every student can be on a FIRST team.

FIRST® LEGO® League introduces STEM to children through fun, exciting hands-on learning. Participants gain real-world problem-solving experience through a guided, global robotics program, helping today's students and teachers build a better future together. FIRST LEGO League's three age-appropriate divisions inspire youth to experiment and grow their critical thinking, coding, and design skills through hands-on STEM learning and robotics centered around a yearly theme.[48]

In grades 9–12, the FIRST Robotics Competition has teams building and programming a robot that will compete with those of other teams. BAE's New Hampshire branch donated $265,000 to FIRST in 2018, and in 2019 the U.S. affiliate of the British-owned BAE Systems corporation initiated a nation-wide annual FIRST Robotics Scholarship and Internship Program for high school seniors.[49]

In Virginia, STEM teachers and volunteers attend the University of Mary Washington Dahlgren campus so they can include in their classes programs based on Sea Perch (an underwater Remotely Operated Vehicle) from Naval Surface Warfare Center Dahlgren Division.[50] Soldiers at Fort Bragg, NC teach in the local public school and mentor students; there are also youth camps on base for troubled local children.[51]

PUBLIC SCHOOLS

Junior Reserve Officers Training Corps (JROTC)

In high schools and middle schools, the DoD's Junior Reserve Officers Training Corps (JROTC) has a curriculum that includes marching, physical training, shooting, and military history and ideology. There are more than 3,000 schools with these programs, representing all service branches.[52]

At a time that schools are trying desperately to discourage violence, the JROTC is teaching students how to kill more effectively. It is also teaching them—in a text that addresses the "Indian menace" that "Fortunately the government policy of pushing the Indians farther West, then wiping them out, was carried out successfully."[53]

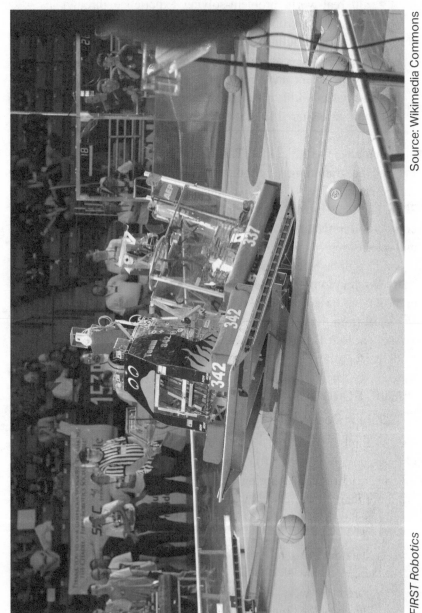

FIRST Robotics

JROTC Cadet Drill

There are more than twelve public high schools that are military academies. Chicago has six, as well as a Middle School Cadet Corps.[54] Parents cannot help but note that unlike the regular high schools, the military academies are well funded and have fine resources while the other public schools are decrepit. Each service branch has its own academies. All students wear uniforms, are in JROTC, and have military classes.[55] In addition, ten thousand children in all Chicago schools are part of JROTC.[56] Very few join the military, yet they will all have been imbued with military doctrine.

Recruitment

The 2001 No Child Left Behind Act requires high schools receiving federal funding to give the military recruiters as much access to campuses and student information as other types of recruiters.[57] The military recruitment budget is over a billion dollars and recruiting is aggressive; the military uses data from websites visited by children.[58] Students are also urged to take the Armed Services Vocational Aptitude Battery, which provides data for recruiters.[59] Parents can opt out, but they often don't know about this provision. Video games are another channel for recruiters. "America's Army was developed by the U.S. military to aid in recruitment and in order to play, you have to register your information through the Army's recruitment website."[60] Adventure vans travel to schools so that the children can participate in military simulation training videos.

Recruiting Van
Source: DoD Army Mission Support Battalion

Subsidies

Public schools near military bases receive several types of subsidies. The U.S. Department of Education gives impact aid to schools, as the government compensates for all federal tax-exempt properties, national parks, Indian lands and others, as well as military installations. The DoD has an additional Impact Aid Program for Military Connected School Districts, and districts with 20% of military-dependent pupils are eligible. These funds are especially welcome in low-income school districts, but the 1% are not neglected. The affluent Town of Lincoln, Massachusetts, has a 2 year (2018–2020) $32 million contract to run Hanscom Air Force Base schools.[61]

The Department of Defense Education Activity has an additional program, awarding grants to military-connected school districts. In 2018, $38 million of these grants were given to 221 schools. One grant, in the state of Washington, funds a program such as this:

> Submariners from *USS Henry M. Jackson* visited third and fourth graders at Brownsville Elementary School as part of a project bringing STEM learning to life. This project will focus on engineering design process, Next Generation Science Standards, and linking English language arts with STEM. Students will work with the Engineering is Elementary kit called "Taking the Plunge: Designing Submersibles." At the end of the module, students will visit their submarine during a field trip.[62]

Another grant that year for $8.8 million went to the National Math Science Initiative. This is a non-governmental organization connected to many STEM organizations, of which the DoD is an important partner. The NMSI features the Army Educational Outreach Program's "Camp Invention," a summer enrichment experience for children in grades K-6. There are over 1,000 such camps; one in Amherst, New Hampshire includes in its description:

> Give your young innovator an unforgettable adventure! All-new, hands-on activities will launch their imagination and get their confidence soaring as they explore STEM fun from the oceans to outer space. Read

more about what your camper will do each day at camp: Campers create a habitat for their own robotic fish — complete with a symbiotic friend — and prototype the next great aquatic innovation to lure in and hook investors at the fish market. Inspired by real space exploration, children construct a Spacepack, engineer an Astro-Arm device, complete gravity-defying cooking challenges, mine asteroids and observe erupting ice volcanoes.[63]

In addition to the economics and adventure connecting the DoD with state and local government, the culture of the military is celebrated in monuments, statues, speeches, parades, school curricula, and artillery.

Central Square, Keene, New Hampshire   Photo: Joan Roelofs

NOTES

The appearance of U.S. Department of Defense (DoD) visual information does not imply or constitute DoD endorsement.

1 Award Profile Grant Summary for Department of Defense (DOD) grant to New Hampshire Office of the Adjutant General (October 1, 2015–September 30, 2017), *USASpending.gov,* https://www.usaspending.gov/award/ASST_NON_W912TF1621001_9700.

2 The Ohio Adjutant General's Department, Ohio Cyber Reserve (OhCR), https://www.ong.ohio.gov/special-units/cyber/ohcr/index.html.

3 Washington Youth Challenge Academy, "About Youth Academy," https://mil.wa.gov/about-youth-academy.

4 Washington Youth Academy Mentor Information, https://mil.wa.gov/asset/61bd09be89bbf.

5 Washington Youth ChalleNGe Academy, https://mil.wa.gov/youth-academy.

6 Sunburst Youth Academy, "Sunburst Mentoring Program," https://www.sunburstadmissions.com/mentor.

7 California Military Institute, https://www.cmicharter.org/5/home.

8 DoD STARBASE: A Department of Defense Youth Program, "Program Description," https://dodstarbase.org/about/.

9 Maj. J. Scott Detweiler, "Vermont National Guard to add Austria as third state partner," Joint Force Headquarters - Vermont National Guard Public Affairs, October 18, 2021, https://www.ang.af.mil/Media/Article-Display/Article/2813147/vermont-national-guard-to-add- austria-as-third-state-partner/.

10 Award Profile Grant Summary for Department of Defense (DOD) grant to The Council of State Governments (September 30, 2013–December 31, 2017), https://www.usaspending.gov/award/ASST_NON_H982101320002_9700.

11 The Council of State Governments, "Policy Projects," https://www.csg.org/policy-projects/.

12 The Council of State Governments, "CSG Announces Selected Professions in Partnership to Develop New Interstate Compacts for Occupational Licensure Portability," *The Current State,* March 17, 2021, https://web.csg.org/tcs/2021/03/17/csg-announces-selected-professions-in-partnership-to-develop-new-interstate-compacts-for-occupational-licensure-portability/.

13 Defense Logistics Agency, "Procurement Technical Assistance Program (PTAP)," https://www.dla.mil/SmallBusiness/PTAP/.

14 *Federal Grants Wire,* "State Memorandum of Agreement Program for the Reimbursement of Technical Services," https://www.federalgrantswire.com/state-memorandum-of-agreement-program-for-the-reimbursement-of-technical-services.html.

15 SERDP-ESTCP, "About SERDP," https://www.serdp-estcp.org/About-SERDP-and-ESTCP/About-SERDP.

16 Jeffrey Foster, "Seed Dispersal Networks and Novel Ecosystem Functioning in Hawaii," SERDP-ESTCP, https://www.serdp-estcp.org/Program-Areas/Resource-Conservation-and-Resiliency/Natural-Resources/Pacific-Island-Ecology-and-Management/RC-2434/(language)/eng-US.

17 Kristina Stinson and Serita Frey, "Restoration of Soil Microbial Function Following Degradation on Department of Defense Lands: Mediating Biological Invasions in a Global Change Context" (SERDP Project RC-2326), Final Report, December 2018, https://apps.dtic.mil/sti/pdfs/AD1069153.pdf.

18 *REPI State Fact Sheets: Maine,* https://www.repi.mil/Portals/44/Documents/State_Packages/Maine_ALLFacts.pdf.

19 Ibid. Also see Chapter 2, Bases and Installations.

20 AnnMarie Harvie, "New England District's Junior Ranger Programs Teach Environmental Stewardship," U.S. Army, May 2, 2018, https://www.army.mil/article/204669/new_england_districts_junior_ranger_programs_teach_environmental_stewardship.

21 "The U.S. Army Corps of Engineers: A Brief History," *U.S. Army Corps of Engineers Headquarters Website,* https://www.usace.army.mil/About/History/Brief-History-of-the-Corps/Introduction/.

22 "Explore USACE Career Opportunities," *U.S. Army Corps of Engineers Headquarters Website,* https://www.usace.army.mil/careers/.

23 U.S. Army Corps of Engineers, *Volunteer Opportunities & Park Attendant Contracts,* https://workamper.com/femp/64521/index.html

24 National Association of Development Organizations, Comprehensive Economic Development Strategy, "CEDS Spotlight: Southeastern Connecticut Enterprise Region," https://www.nado.org/ceds-spotlight-southeastern-connecticut-enterprise-region/.

25 Washington State Department of Commerce, "Protecting our freedoms," *CHOOSE Washington,* http://choosewashingtonstate.com/why-washington/our-key-sectors/military-defense/.

26 Washington Economic Development Association, "About WEDA," https://wedaonline.org/about-weda/.

27 Jessie Stensland, "Group Sues Over Navy Training in State Parks," *Whidbey News-Times,* March 9, 2021, https://www.whidbeynewstimes.com/news/group-sues-over-navy-training-in-state-parks/.

28 New Hampshire Aerospace & Defense Export Consortium (NHADEC), "Members," https://nhadec.com/members/.

29 Association of Defense Communities, https://defensecommunities.org.

30 U.S. Department of Defense, Office of Local Defense Community Cooperation, "DOD Approves $50 Million in Grants Under Defense Community Infrastructure Pilot Program," September 17, 2020, https://oldcc.gov/dod-approves-50-million-grants-under-defense-community-infrastructure-pilot-program.

31 Chris Duyos, "Sharing Produce and Promoting Health in the Peace State," Association of Defense Communities, November 2021, https://defensecommunities.org/wp-content/uploads/2021/11/2021-Coastal-Georgia-Farmers-Market-Story.pdf.

32 "Weapons Investments by Various Countries and States," World Beyond War, https://worldbeyondwar.org/weapons-investments-by-various-countries-and-states/.

33 Teachers' Retirement System of the City of New York, Investment Portfolios, June 30, 2020, https://www.trsnyc.org/memberportal/WebContent/publications/financialReports/investmentPortfolio2020.

34 ICAN, "New York City Joins ICAN Cities Appeal," December 9, 2021, https://www.icanw.org/new_york_city_joins_ican_cities_appeal.

35 Divest from the War Machine, "Victories," https://www.divestfromwarmachine. org/victories.

36 CodePink, "Burlington, Vermont Divests from Weapons Manufacturers!" July 12, 2021, https://www.codepink.org/burlington_divest_victory.

37 Arnie Alpert, "Commentary: Abolish draft registration – don't expand it to include women," *New Hampshire Bulletin,* December 22, 2021 https:// newhampshirebulletin.com/2021/12/22/commentary-abolish-draft-registration-dont-expand-it-to-include-women/.

38 Wayne McElrath and Sarah Turberville, "Poisoning Our Police: How the Militarization Mindset Threatens Constitutional Rights and Public Safety," *POGO,* June 9, 2020, https://www.pogo.org/analysis/2020/06/poisoning-our-police-how-the-militarization-mindset-threatens-constitutional-rights-and-public-safety/.

39 Max Proulx, "Reports on Keene's Bearcat may soon end," *The Keene Sentinel,* December 11, 2015, https://www.sentinelsource.com/news/local/reports-on-keenes-bearcat-may-soon-end/article_c6be910a-fa94-59ac-8abd-d5b133a60647.html

40 Simone Weichselbaum, Beth Schwartzapfel and Tom Meagher, "When Warriors Put on the Badge," *The Marshall Project,* March 30, 2017, https://www. themarshallproject.org/2017/03/30/when-warriors-put-on-the-badge.

41 Ibid.

42 California State University, Monterey Bay, "1862, July 2–12 Stat. 503, Act Donating Public Land For Colleges," *Digital Commons @ CSUMB,* June 15, 2016, https://digitalcommons.csumb.edu/cgi/viewcontent. cgi?article=1012&context=hornbeck_usa_2_d.

43 "Land-Grab Universities," *High Country News* (March 2020), https://www. landgrabu.org/.

44 William M. Arkin and Alexa O'Brien, "The Most Militarized Universities in America: A VICE News Investigation," *VICE News,* November 6, 2015, https:// www.vice.com/en/article/j59g5b/the-most-militarized-universities-in-america-a-vice-news-investigation.

45 Divest from the War Machine, "End the Portland State University Boeing Internship Program" (petition), https://www.divestfromwarmachine.org/ noboeingpsu.

46 BAE Systems, "BAE Systems partners with University of New Hampshire on STEM program for high school students," October 3, 2018, https://www. baesystems.com/en/article/bae-systems-partners-with-university-of-new-hampshire-on-stem-program-for-high-school-students.

47 U.S. Department of Defense, "Dr. Robert M. Gates, Former Secretary of Defense," https://www.defense.gov/About/Biographies/Biography/Article/602797/.

48 "FIRST ENERGIZE, presented by Qualcomm," https://info.firstinspires.org/ firstforward?utm_source=adwords&utm_term=%2Bfirst%20%2Brobotics%20 %2Bcompetition&utm_medium=ppc&utm_campaign.

49 BAE Systems, "Billion-Dollar impact on 2018 New Hampshire economy," March 27, 2019, https://www.baesystems.com/en/article/billion-dollar-impact-on-2018-new-hampshire-economy.

50 Naval Sea Systems Command, "NSWC Dahlgren Mentors Inspire Middle and High School 'SeaPerch' Teachers," December 20, 2019, https://www.navsea.navy. mil/Media/News/SavedNewsModule/Article/2045727/nswc-dahlgren-mentors-inspire-middle-and-high-school-seaperch-teachers/.

51 Catherine Lutz, *Homefront* (Boston: Beacon Press, 2001), 221.

52 Congressional Research Service, "Defense Primer: Junior Reserve Officers' Training Corps (JROTC)," *In Focus,* updated June 15, 2022, https://fas.org/sgp/crs/natsec/IF11313.pdf.

53 Sam Smith, "The Militarization of American Life," *Progressive Review* (March 1996), https://samsmitharchives.wordpress.com/1996/04/21/the-militarization-of-american-life/.

54 "Middle School Cadet Corps," Wikipedia, https://en.wikipedia.org/wiki/Middle_School_Cadet_Corps.

55 *USA Today,* June 4, 2009.

56 Sarah Jaffe, "Trump's Austerity Budget Increases Military Recruiters' Power to Prey on Youth," *NNOMY,* March 24, 2017, http://nnomy.org/index.php/427-flexicontent/articles/733-trump-s-austerity-budget-increases-military-recruiters-power-to-prey-on-youth.

57 Seth Kershner and Scott Harding, "Commentary: Do Military Recruiters Belong in Schools?," *Education Week,* October 28, 2015, http://ew.edweek.org/nxtbooks/epe/ew_10282015/index.php?startid=20#/p/20.

58 "The [Wall Street] Journal reported that N2H2 (NTWO), the leading provider of Web-filtering services to U.S. K-12 schools, is telling the department [DoD] which websites students visit most while at school." Jeffrey Benner, "The Army Is Watching Your Kid," *Wired,* January 29, 2001, https://www.wired.com/2001/01/the-army-is-watching-your-kid/.

59 ASVAB Career Exploration Program, http://www.asvabprogram.com/.

60 NNOMY, Resources: "Militarized Gaming as Recruitment Tools," https://nnomy.org/en/resources/downloads/youth-violence/militarized-gaming-as-recruitment-tools.html.

61 Award Profile Contract Summary for Department of Defense (DOD) award to Town of Lincoln (June 29, 2018–June 30, 2020), https://www.usaspending.gov/award/68936925.

62 Department of Defense Education Activity (DoDEA), https://www.dodea.edu/Partnership/grants.cfm.

63 National Inventors Hall of Fame, program search result: "Amherst Middle School: Week 1 - Camp Invention: Explore," https://invent-web.ungerboeck.com/programsearch/moreinfo.aspx?event=36924.

CHAPTER SEVEN

WHAT CAN BE DONE

There are many people and organizations doing good work in an effort to diminish the power of the warfare state, reduce the risk of nuclear annihilation, and promote a world of peace and justice. These efforts make the extent and the implications of the military industrial complex more visible. But many look away, and the mountain is huge to move.

WHAT YOU CAN DO TO HELP BREAK THE SILENCE

1. Breaking the silence is feasible.

Learn about the military industrial complex, the policies it supports, and the consequences of its preparations and operations. Then talk about it both informally and in presentations to your community. Information is most willingly received by those with whom you have some connection: family, neighbor, hobby buddy, colleague, or congregation. In addition, local organizations frequently looking for speakers provide another opportunity. Remind anti-poverty, human rights, and environmental organizations about how militarization exacerbates their concerns. Nongovernmental organizations' military connections are particularly obscure and need to be brought to their attention, as some may indeed be unwitting of same.

The mainstream media, local and national, may be silent, tell only part of the story, or serve as a channel for military propaganda. Write letters to the editor and op-eds for your local newspaper. Use the Comments section of online news outlets wherever possible. Utilize diverse sources of information to lend more authority to your contribution. Among the most useful, all online, are these:

- National Priorities Project,
- Center for Defense Information,
- Center for International Policy,

- Federation of American Scientists,
- Watson Institute Costs of War Project,
- *Antiwar.com*,
- *TomDispatch*,
- *CovertAction Quarterly*,
- Stockholm International Peace Research Institute,
- *Black Agenda Report*, and the
- Quincy Institute for Responsible Statecraft, a new think tank incorporating both progressives and anti-interventionist conservatives.

International organizations and news sources are readily available in English online and may be very informative.

Those who belong to community organizations are more likely to be influential. They can then advocate against receiving donations from military corporations, investing funds in portfolios with military contractor stocks, or appointing board members who are current employees of the DoD or weapons contractors. Veterans' organizations are OK; many are aghast at the horrors of war, and most are very well informed about the activities of the military. Even if these appeals are not successful, members will be awakened to the pervasiveness of militarization—they are often unaware of the extent and diversity of entanglements between the military and civilian life, even in areas where they themselves are active. Join local political party committees, which are generally very welcoming to new members.

2.   Contact your Congresspeople or President, or sign petitions online.

An organization that makes this very easy is RootsAction, which will forward your message (or one that they have composed) to your representatives.[1] You can also send the appeals to your friends, post them on a Facebook or other media page, and inform your community in a letter to the editor of a local news source.

3. **Join and work with antiwar organizations, or if that is not practical, send a donation.**

Let people know of your affiliations so as to increase the visibility of the peace movement. Some antiwar organizations that are focused on the most vital problems include:

Code Pink. This organization fearlessly seeks the truth behind international conflicts. It supports a coalition advocating divestment from weapons industries.[2]

The **Divest From the War Machine** website enables individuals, organizations, churches, and pensioners to learn of nuclear and other weapon makers in their investment funds.[3] This project is focused especially on state and local government workers' pension funds, which are loaded with military stocks. Divestment is unlikely to cause bankruptcy to Lockheed et al, but it is extremely helpful in bringing visibility to the MIC's economic power and its connections to the interests of ordinary people, including progressive activists.

World Beyond War. This very active peace organization has international chapters. It is concerned with many aspects of militarization, including divestment, conversion of military to civilian industries, promotion of diplomacy and international law, and effective enforcement of laws against war. Its approach is described in *A Global Security System,* which explains three strategies for ending war: 1) demilitarizing security, 2) managing conflicts without violence, and 3) creating a culture of peace.[4] WBW is part of the Divest Chicago from the War Machine Coalition to remove the City's pension funds from weapons manufacturers and military contractors.

The **International Campaign to Abolish Nuclear Weapons (ICAN)** has worked to promote and obtain ratification by governments of the Treaty on the Prohibition of Nuclear Weapons. The Treaty has had enough ratifications to come into force as international law. However, no nuclear weapon-armed power has ratified it, insofar as the treaty calls for nuclear weapon-armed states to take steps towards nuclear disarmament. ICAN's ongoing efforts include generating ideas for how citizens can pressure their governments to ratify the treaty and respect the provisions. These include prohibiting any help from a signatory to the nuclear weapons operations of any nation.[5]

The **National Network Opposing the Militarization of Youth (NNOMY).** This group engages in counter recruitment work and its members include activists from religious groups, veterans who have experienced the horrors of war, and parents and students working to de-militarize schools.[6]

Veterans For Peace. This group has over 120 chapters, some international, and holds permanent Nongovernmental

Organization status at the United Nations. It is concerned with "the causes of war; redirecting the military budget towards human needs, pushing for the global abolition of nuclear weapons, and eliminating the ability of corporations to profit from war."[7] It is the sponsor of:

- **War Industry Resisters Network**

- **Military Families Speak Out,** which describes itself as "[an] organization of military families across the U.S. and around the world who have a loved one who has served in the military since 9-11. Our membership includes Gold Star Families. We oppose the wars in Iraq and Syria, and speak out against other unjust military interventions.

  "As families with loved ones who were or are in the military, we have both a unique voice and role to play in speaking out. It is our loved ones who are, have been, or will be on the frontlines. It is our loved ones who are risking injury and death. It is our loved ones who are returning scarred both physically and emotionally.

  "The mission of Military Families Speak Out is to advocate for all U.S. troops to leave Iraq and Afghanistan now and to speak out against unjust military interventions. MFSO supports policies that utilize diplomacy over military force. We support the troops and work hard to ensure that their needs are met while deployed and when they return home."[8]

About Face: Veterans Against the War, self-described: "We are Post-9/11 service members and veterans organizing to end a foreign policy of permanent war and the use of military weapons, tactics, and values in communities across the country. As people intimately familiar with the inner workings of the world's largest military, we use our knowledge and experiences to expose the truth about these conflicts overseas and the growing militarization in the United States."[9]

There are many others doing important work, including:

- American Friends Service Committee
- Institute for Policy Studies
- Peace Action
- United for Peace and Justice
- U.S. Peace Council
- War Resisters League
- Women's International League for Peace and Freedom
- Black Alliance for Peace
- Campaign for Peace, Disarmament and Common Security

Some of these are affiliates of international coalitions, such as **No to War–No to NATO**, a network of hundreds of peace groups throughout the world, 14 of which are United States organizations.[10] Perhaps they could heighten their effectiveness by forming a continuing council, with representatives from all groups and invited social scientists, to figure out how to end war and demilitarize the world.

Even if you lack the time or inclination for public engagement, you can send a donation. Most antiwar groups and websites have a feature enabling supporters' donations. Your privacy will be respected if requested, and many such organizations also enable tax deductions.

A GREEN NEW DEAL

We need to heal society and our land not only from war and its preparation, but from its many ills. The idea of a Green New Deal is in the air. It would need to be comprehensive, in accordance with the key values of the original U.S. Green movement of the 1980s, such as ecological wisdom, social justice, nonviolence, decentralization and respect for diversity.[11] The Green movement was not able to propel the needed massive transition. This remains a matter of the greatest urgency and yet is a thorny puzzle. One of several organizations now fathoming this is "The Great Transition Initiative," but much more work on this matter is required,[12] as an instance, well-funded think tanks engaging physical and social scientists, activists, representatives of diverse occupations, cultures, indigenous peoples, and foreign wisdom—and even some industrialists.

If we are to wean our country from militarization and the military permeation of our economy, we need to begin work not only on transitioning from military spending, but also to describe and promote a preferable alternative economy, politics, and culture. Here are some of the problems that must be addressed in the United States:

- the extreme level of violence (rare in so-called advanced societies),
- injustice and inequality,
- the unhappiness of youth,
- addiction to drugs such as alcohol, opioids, cannabis, and anti-depressants,
- poor mental and physical health, declining life expectancy,
- destruction of the environment,
- crumbling public and private infrastructure, including shabby and unhealthy schools and homes, even those of the affluent,
- numerous deaths by fire, uncommon in most civilized nations,
- the meaninglessness, hazards, and wastefulness of much work,
- the economic role of drugs, pornography, and crime,
- the exploitation of workers, especially the undocumented, who are deemed essential to our economy,
- the militarization of higher education,
- the oppression of student debt,
- aggressive and violent foreign policies.

CREATING A PEACE CULTURE
A National Service Program

We must take into account real human beings and their psychology. William James' 1910 essay, "The Moral Equivalent of War" had some good suggestions that can be readily updated, with this trenchant warning as to the difficulty of the project:

> The war against war is going to be no holiday excursion or camping party. The military feelings are too deeply grounded to abdicate their place among our ideals until better substitutes are offered than the glory and shame that

come to nations as well as to individuals from the ups and downs of politics and the vicissitudes of trade.[13]

His proposal for a substitute for war, a "moral equivalent of war," makes explicit the issue:

> Men now are proud of belonging to a conquering nation, and without a murmur they lay down their persons and their wealth, if by so doing they may fend off subjection. But who can be sure that other aspects of one's country may not, with time and education and suggestion enough, come to be regarded with similarly effective feelings of pride and shame?

Why should men not someday feel that it is worth a blood-tax to belong to a collectivity superior in any ideal respect? Why should they not blush with indignant shame if the community that owns them is vile in any way whatsoever?[14]

James embraced the conscription of youth but proposed instead that it have more desirable, alternative objectives:

> If now—and this is my idea—there were, instead of military conscription, a conscription of the whole youthful population to form for a certain number of years a part of the army enlisted against Nature, the injustice [of inequality in toil] would tend to be evened out, and numerous other goods to the commonwealth would follow.[15]

The older ideal that democracy requires equality in "toil" has faded and has been replaced by the goals of social democracy—greater equality in living standards and consumption—but it is worthy of reconsideration. Nevertheless, James' "youth army" would surely require some modification in the light of today's values. He ignored the psychological needs of women, whose role has often been that of supporting the male warriors. A civilian corps would need to be inclusive. James was also concerned that such a civilian construction would not be considered heroic enough to be a moral equivalent of war. Today both ecological devastation and rampant, planet-threatening militarism require superhuman efforts. Finally, we wouldn't want a corps that was enlisted "against Nature," but one that worked with Nature and appropriate technology to achieve the best outcomes for humans and the planet.

James' idea lives on in proposals for a civilian national service that would expand the Americorps program. Recently, Senator Jack Reed, Democrat of Rhode Island, introduced the ACTION for National Service Act.[16] He spoke of its merits:

> Finding common cause through service is how we will overcome the major challenges of our time, from recovering from the COVID-19 pandemic to addressing inequality to strengthening civil society and democratic institutions to leaving a healthy, resilient planet to future generations. . . . Our legislation calls for a historic expansion of the number of service opportunities and an increased investment in those who serve. The ACTION for National Service Act will honor our national value of service, while addressing the barriers that limit citizens' opportunities to serve. Our legislation will set us on a path to 1 million national service positions within 10 years. It will increase the educational award so that an individual completing 2 full years of service will earn the equivalent of 4 years of the average in-state tuition at a public college or university.[17]

Although it would be a major step toward equality, there is little support for a draft, or universal service, especially on the anarchist-inflected left, but also on the right, which complains about China's social credit system. Nevertheless, even a voluntary service program would provide a constructive alternative to military recruitment. Young people who now seek the benefits, training, and adventure of military service would enlist in such a national service program. They could gain the satisfactions of patriotism, service, and comradeship, and come away with fewer mental health problems than are common with lethality training and combat service. They could gain a reasonably priced education or vocational training and become an influence in their communities for the values and accomplishments of civilian services. Those with a need to perform heroic deeds would find appropriate challenges given the condition of the nation.

Young children also need to be exposed to a culture of peace, justice, and equality. Those of all backgrounds are perpetrators and victims of violence, huddled in gangs or bullying others, glued to violent video games, battered in warlike team sports, awash with drugs, isolated, depressed, sedentary, feeling inadequate, or just plain unhappy. Their social and cultural lives are already being directed or influenced by adults: schools, churches, industries, and organizations, as well as parents. Those who argue for children's "freedom" usually mean the freedom of parents or other adults to impose their values.

We need healthful, affirming, constructive activity that is inclusive—no child left out. Current youth organizations are often closely connected to the military industrial complex, and/or commercial interests. To promote peaceful co-existence, children of all backgrounds and abilities would need to be enrolled; respect for diversity needs to start early in life. Activities could include games and arts, along with environmental restoration, infrastructure repair, and social services, in ways that were fun, instructive, and constructive. A minor cultural change that could influence children positively would be the designation of a more illuminating national anthem to replace one glorifying bombing and war.

CONVERSION TO A CIVILIAN ECONOMY

The government is already heavily engaged in or subsidizing much of the economy, but not as part of an overall plan that would further the ideals of peace, justice, and environmental protection. The gigantic funds now going to (or through) the military would easily support a conversion to a civilian economy producing "for use" rather than for profit or merely providing jobs. A green new deal would, among other objectives, consider the wellbeing of all on the planet, perhaps inspired by a provision of the Universal Declaration of Human Rights:

> Everyone has the right to a standard of living adequate for the health and well-being of himself [sic] and of his family, including food, clothing, housing and medical care and necessary social services, and the right to security in the event of unemployment, sickness, disability,

widowhood, old age or other lack of livelihood in circumstances beyond his control. (Article 25)

A government department could be created for Civilian Infrastructure, including waterways and green transportation, absorbing the Army Engineers and separating their useful functions from the military's lethality mission. Environmental protection might be promoted to a major department, engaging in remediation as well as setting and enforcing standards for all activities, economic, recreational and cultural.

The Agriculture Department needs to oversee a total transformation of our food, fiber, and forestry systems. Here a national civilian service could play a large role. In the U.S. as well as other industrialized societies, agricultural labor is mostly performed by immigrants or foreign contract workers. The work is hard, the workers have few rights, and they are silenced by their status:

> It is an open secret that the vast majority of people who harvest America's food are undocumented immigrants, mainly from Mexico, many of them decades-long residents of the United States. Often the parents of American-born children, they have lived for years with the cloud of deportation hanging over their households.[18]

In addition, due to shortages of farm workers, accentuated by Covid, farm operators are increasingly using prison labor.

The exploitation of labor isn't the only problem with our agricultural system. Monoculture, chemical and waste pollution, fossil fuel use and emissions, unhealthful products, massive imports of food easily raised locally, enormous agribusiness land use destroying peopled communities, animal abuse, child labor, hunger, food wasted at all stages, and so on. The majority of farmers, many hardworking, cannot support themselves by their farm operations, and must find outside jobs or have another source of income. A healthier, more local and plant-based diet would require even more labor, more barely paid small organic farmers, and food prices unacceptable even to middle income consumers, under our "market" system. Instead of the billions now spent by the government subsidizing large-scale commodity producers, we could reconstruct the system so that it respects and nourishes. Immigrants, many of whom have superior agricultural knowledge and skills, could still be part of the system as national service volunteers or professional farm managers. However, all would be protected by civil service standards, with adequate benefits, housing, safety measures, and short workdays.

A Civilian Goods Department might plan for replacement of most products we now import, bringing jobs back into both rural and urban communities throughout the nation. In addition to returning manufacturing to our shores, it would be dedicated to researching the best technology for creating useful, well-designed, durable and affordable items, with the least harmful impact on the environment or hazards to workers, communities, and consumers. There is ample space here for conversion of military-related industry to civilian purposes. Such an economy would not be dependent on production and export of weapons, or bases and other military installations and activities. Current weapons producers that also make civilian products would most easily be integrated into a civilian economy. Perhaps the huge brains affiliated with DARPA could be transferred to a CARPA, Civilian Advanced Research Products Agency, to help figure it out.

In addition, spending previously allocated to the military to address health, housing, welfare, education, and culture of troops, base communities, and veterans could be provided directly, without the military intermediary, to relevant government departments. While the VA health system and the GI Bill promoted much greater equality, it was mostly white male veterans who benefitted, and the political strength of those seeking universal provision was greatly diluted.

We could maintain an appropriately scaled military department and budget rather than one that is more than the next nine countries combined,[19] one addressing actual issues of national defense rather than bent on foreign expansion and aggression, and with a strong commitment to peaceful solution of disputes.

All government departments and independent agencies would be attuned to the objectives of the green new deal, e.g., Justice, Commerce, State, Homeland Security, and USAID, TVA, and CIA. Enlarged civilian departments for social services, housing, health, and education could include work for the youth service contingent. They might aid in caring for the young, disabled, and old; work in community cafeterias (as restaurant workers are another group often exploited and increasingly scarce); and serve in necessary jobs that are scarce of applicants. The young people might discover their future careers through their service, or they could proceed to higher education for other choices.

Like every other country in the world, the U.S. economy is "mixed," with both private and public enterprise. The proposals indicated above would change the mix, but they would not signal a seismic transition from "capitalist" to "socialist." National, state, local, municipal, community, workers' or consumers' cooperative, or private enterprise would exist as appropriate to the service or product. Modern technology can enable remote self-sufficient industrial and agricultural communities, among other configurations. Government economic departments could still issue contracts for goods and services, and grants to states could bring them into the transition; the economy as before would be "mixed." Generous provisions for retraining workers and possible relocation would be required to make the transition acceptable, as workers rarely vote to shut down their own industries even if harmful to themselves and others. A peaceful world would include the removal of foreign military bases and installations, and drastic shrinkage of the number and size of our domestic ones. Veterans and former base workers here and abroad would find suitable employment in the civilian economy.

A retreat from economic globalization is not "isolationism." There is plenty of land here, and even usable infrastructure in our ghost and rusting towns. We can welcome immigrants, who bring energy, health, and skills that can help to revitalize the nation. However, curtailing our military and corporate globalization will reduce the number who are forced to migrate from war torn countries, such as those of Central America.

INTERNATIONAL RELATIONS

There have long existed many mechanisms for resolving disputes among nations without war, including international law, diplomacy, mediation, conciliation, international courts, and international organizations. The problem is that they must be used and made effective. While NATO claims to advocate peaceful settlement, stating in its founding document that "Whereas the parties to the North Atlantic Treaty, under Article I of that treaty, have undertaken 'to settle any international disputes in which they may be involved by peaceful means in such a manner that international peace and security and justice are not endangered...'"[20] this applies, and in theory only, to disputes among its own members. The creation of NATO, its out of area wars beginning with Yugoslavia, and its expansion, now even more dangerously increasing, has been met with the vast silence of the U.S. public.

The very existence of NATO contradicted the UN Charter, which held out hope for countering aggressive nations by means of collective security and was based on the common belief that military alliances were a major cause of war. The people of the United States (indeed, of the world) would be safer and their lands cleaner if the U.S. closed its overseas bases (and most of the domestic ones), ended its regime changes, war games, proxy wars, and bombings, and began to dissolve NATO and its partnerships.

> We might take a leaf from the constitutional provision we imposed on Japan after World War II; Renunciation of war. Article 9. Aspiring sincerely to an international peace based on justice and order, the Japanese people forever renounce war as a sovereign right of the nation and the threat or use of force as means of settling international disputes.[21]

There is plenty of challenging work to do healing the planet.

THE FINAL WORD

The millions sheltered under our thick insecurity blanket, including the enlistees under the most prickly part of it, are not to blame. A very few people may be thrilled by the idea of wreaking death and destruction, but most are just trying to earn a living, raise their families, and keep their organization or rust belt afloat. Those engaged in weapons production may prefer constructive work or income from civilian sources. Still, many have been indoctrinated to believe that militarism is normal and necessary. Those who see the necessity of change for planetary survival, justice, and sanity need to become aware of all the ways that the military-industrial-congressional-almost everything-complex is being sustained. This book has documented part of the picture; there is, unfortunately, much more. Once this understanding is achieved, there remains the difficult work of making such a transition happen, in view of militarization's political strength in the U.S. and much of the world. Our political system, despite its well-publicized and expensive elections, does not afford citizens much democratic control over policies, and hardly any over foreign policy.

Military organization can get *things* done, without waiting for someone to decide that a profit can be made or the need to balance costs and benefits (to put it mildly). That type of organization can also promote cooperation, respect for diversity, and comradery. The problem is with the *things:* superpower dominance, regime change, a multitude of military bases, bombing countries back to the stone age.... If the Department of Defense were reduced to protecting against actual threats, focusing on defense rather than aggression, there would be fewer threats, and resources aplenty for necessary domestic reconstruction. A Green New Deal, including national service, could be the first step in "civilianizing" our nation. In addition to preventing it from looming disaster, it could enhance our own and the world's prospects for health, justice, and sustainability. If we could divert the same trillions the government is already injecting into the economy to civilian purposes, we could repair the environment, provide everyone a fine standard of living, and work for peace on earth.

NOTES

1 RootsAction, https://www.rootsaction.org.
2 "The Coalition," Divest from the War Machine, https://www. divestfromwarmachine.org/coalition.
3 Weapon Free Funds, https://www.weaponfreefunds.org.
4 Kent Shifferd, Patrick Hiller (authors), and Phill Gittins (ed.), *A Global Security System: An Alternative to War* (World Beyond War, 2020), available at "The AGSS," World Beyond War, https://worldbeyondwar.org/alternative.
5 ICAN, https://www.icanw.org.
6 "Community Action," The National Network Opposing the Militarization of Youth (NNOMY), https://nnomy.org/en/groups-campaigns-activities/community-action. html.
7 Veterans For Peace, https://www.veteransforpeace.org/.
8 Military Families Speak Out, https://militaryfamiliesspeakout.com/
9 About Face, https://aboutfaceveterans.org/
10 "About Us," No to War, No to NATO Network, https://www.no-to-nato.org/about-us-no-to-war-no-to-nato-network/.
11 Joan Roelofs, *Greening Cities: Building Just and Sustainable Communities* (Blue Ridge Summit, Penn.: Rowman & Littlefield, 1996), 2.
12 Great Transition Initiative, https://www.greattransition.org/
13 William James, "The Moral Equivalent of War," *Popular Science Monthly,* Vol. 77, October 1910 (based on a talk given in 1906), accessed at *Wikisource,* https://en.wikisource.org/wiki/Popular_Science_Monthly/Volume_77/October_1910/The_Moral_Equivalent_of_War.
14 Ibid.
15 Ibid.
16 S.3622 - ACTION for National Service Act was introduced by Senator Reed on 02/09/2022 in the 117th Congress (2021–2022).
17 "Proceedings and Debates of the 117th Congress, Second Session, *Congressional Record,* Vol. 168, No. 26 (Feb. 9, 2022), https://www.congress.gov/congressional-record/2022/02/09/senate-section/article/S613-3.
18 Miriam Jordan, "Farmworkers, Mostly Undocumented, Become 'Essential' During Pandemic," *The New York Times* (April 2, 2020), https://www.nytimes.com/2020/04/02/us/coronavirus-undocumented-immigrant-farmworkers-agriculture.html.
19 Peter G. Peterson Foundation, "U.S. Defense Spending Compared to Other Countries," May 11, 2022, https://www.pgpf.org/chart-archive/0053_defense-comparison.
20 North Atlantic Treaty Organization (NATO), "Resolution on the Peaceful Settlement of Disputes and Differences between Members of the North Atlantic Treaty Organization," 11 Dec. 1956–14 Dec. 1956, https://www.nato.int/cps/en/natohq/official_texts_17482.htm.
21 Prime Minister of Japan and His Cabinet, *The Constitution of Japan* (promulgated on November 3, 1946; came into effect on May 3, 1947), https://japan.kantei.go.jp/constitution_and_government_of_japan/constitution_e.html.

INDEX